Rethinking the university

MANCHESTER
UNIVERSITY PRESS

Rethinking the university

Leverage and deconstruction

Simon Wortham

Manchester University Press

Manchester and New York

distributed exclusively in the USA by St. Martin's Press

Published by Manchester University Press
Oxford Road, Manchester M13 9NR, UK
and Room 400, 175 Fifth Avenue, New York, NY 10010, USA
http://www.man.ac.uk/mup

Distributed exclusively in the USA by
St. Martin's Press, Inc., 175 Fifth Avenue, New York, NY 10010, USA

Distributed exclusively in Canada by
UBC Press, University of British Columbia, 6344 Memorial Road
Vancouver, BC, Canada V6T 1Z2

British Library Cataloguing-in-Publication Data
A catalogue record for this book is available from the British Library

Library of Congress Cataloging-in-Publication Data applied for

ISBN 0 7190 5629 2 *hardback*

First published 1999

06 05 04 03 02 01 00 99   10 9 8 7 6 5 4 3 2 1

Typeset by Helen Skelton, London
Printed in Great Britain by Bookcraft (Bath) Ltd, Midsomer Norton

For Lisa

Contents

Acknowledgements

Versions of parts of this book have been published in the following journals, and are reprinted with permission: 'The "glasse" of majesty: reflections on new historicism and cultural materialism', *Angelaki*, 2:2 (1996); 'Multiple submissions and little scrolls of parchment: censorship, knowledge, and the academy', *New Literary History*, 28:3 (1997); 'Bringing criticism to account: economy, exchange and cultural theory', *Economy and Society*, 26:3 (1997); 'Surviving theory, "*as if* I[t] were dead": Derrida and interdisciplinarity', *new formations*, 34 (1998).

I would like to thank Gary Hall, Geoffrey Hemstedt and Graham MacPhee for their interest in my work over the years, and Matthew Frost at Manchester University Press for his enthusiasm and his support in the publication of this book. Thanks also to Jo Acres and Jamie Freeman for listening, and to Lisa Wortham for everything else.

Walking on two feet

The aim of this book, baldly put, is to explore and develop key critical debates in the humanities in recent times (concerning, for example, postmodernism, new historicism, political criticism, cultural studies, interdisciplinarity, and deconstruction) in the context of the legitimation crisis widely felt to be facing academic institutions, using Derrida's idea of leverage in the university as a critical point of departure. In particular, by focusing on this idea my concern is to try to account for the malaise in the university by linking critical developments, discourses and debates in the modern humanities to a problem of the institution itself; finding within these discourses and debates the very dimensions of the institution's predicament: economic, political, ideological, but also, inseparably, intellectual.

In the last few years there have been several important studies of the university published in Britain and the US by critics owing a debt to deconstruction and to Derrida's work on the question of the university. Based on the proceedings of a conference held at the University of Alabama in 1987, *Logomachia: The Conflict of the Faculties*, edited by Richard Rand, appeared in 1992. This brought together a number of essays by such noted critics as Timothy Bahti, Alan Bass, Peggy Kamuf, John Llewelyn and Robert Young, grouping their work around Derrida's enormously influential reading of Kant's hitherto neglected text *The Conflict of the Faculties* (1798), in which Derrida raises the question of the university's founding, its institution and orientation. Derrida's essay 'Mochlos' was in fact first delivered as a paper at Columbia University in 1980 and can therefore be placed alongside another article entitled 'The principle of reason: the university in the eyes of its pupils', which appeared in the American publication *Diacritics* in 1983. Here Derrida takes direction from an essay by James Siegel, 'Academic work: the view from Cornell', published two years earlier in the same journal. Once more, Derrida's discussion stems from the question of the university's foundations and, in turn, the problem of orientation that this raises. These two papers can usefully be put together, along with 'Sendoffs' (originally published in 1982, the English translation appearing in *Yale French Studies* 77 in 1990) and other texts on the College International de Philosophie, inasmuch as the question of the university institution forms an *explicit* interest for Derrida around this period. (Of course, it would be difficult to find a text by him that was not in some way concerned with the question of the institution). Included in *Logomachia* in English translation as an 'indispensable point of reference', 'Mochlos' – by now over a decade old – thus became the focus of renewed interest in the issue of (re)thinking the university.

From 1993 onwards, meanwhile, a number of important articles on the university were published by the up-and-coming critic Bill Readings, forming the backbone of his book *The University in Ruins*, published posthumously in 1996. Against the backdrop of a close examination of the concept and role of the university historically, Readings explores the institutional plight of the 'posthistorical' university of excellence, now devoid of social mission or function with the decline of the nation-state and the globalisation of late capitalism, and therefore subject to a process of 'dereferentialisation' with regard to any idea or organising principle of reason or culture that hitherto had served as keystones of the modern university. Readings shows how the German Idealists from Schiller to Humboldt substituted a concept and a content of culture for Kant's notion of reason as the regulatory ideal of the modern university and the *ratio* between disciplines. In this way, Readings suggests, they assigned a more explicitly political role to the modern university as the unifying institution in which the sum of knowledge and the cultivation of character (*Bildung*) were tied to the development of the ideological lineaments of modern nation-states.

In Germany in particular this shift from reason to culture in the formation of the modern university provided a way to reconcile, as Readings puts it, 'ethnic tradition and statist rationality',[1] so as to overcome the otherwise potentially menacing interplay between reason and republican will in the institutional model derived from Kantian thought while at the same time establishing the conditions to realise the essence of *Volk* in the very plan of the university. For Readings, traces of the strong connection between modern institutions of education and republicanism have none the less remained in the US and are perhaps most visible in heated debates about canonicity. 'The canon matters in the United States,' he writes, 'because the determination of the canon is taken to be the result of an exercise of republican will. The autonomous *choice* of a canon, rather than submission to the blind weight of tradition, parallels the choice of a government rather than submission to hereditary monarchy' (p. 16). Here, the traditional content of the American canon is less important than its function as the epitome of the promissory structure of American republicanism itself, so that the continuous processes of selection and reselection with regard to a canonical literature go hand in hand with the democratic social contract imagined to exist between the people and the state. However, the specifically literary turn given to the interplay of university and nation-state from the late nineteenth century onwards in Britain (under the influence of Newman, Arnold, Newbolt and Leavis, among others) established the conditions for a somewhat different institutionalisation of literature, as a discipline, in terms of its production of 'an organic vision of the possibility of a unified national culture' (p. 16). Here, the university as the uppermost institution of education was stridently reasserted in terms of the sacralised and totemic role hitherto accorded the church, and after Newbolt's 1921 HMSO report, 'The Teaching of English in England', literature – as not just a cultural reserve but also a discipline – assumed almost a religious value within a now increasingly secular modern nation-state. The supposedly organic and unifying connection cemented in the English university between a national literature and a national culture, imagined as a way to stave off urban, industrial anarchy in the latter half of the last century and subsequently to revivify and rebuild nationhood particularly between the wars, therefore very much accentuated ethnic tradition (specifically, that of 'Englishness') over popular will.

Nevertheless, as the ideological apparatus of the nation-state weakens in view of the apparently irresistible rise of transnational corporations with their ideologically colourless logics and practices of managerial excellence, for Readings the picture changes decisively within and across various national models of the university. Once the subject of university pedagogy (the student) ceases to be imagined as metonymically the embodiment of generalised social, national or ethnic values (now in decline in an age of global capital) the university faces a legitimation crisis which he suggests it tries to disregard by embracing corporate-style management and bureacratic rationality, now thinking of itself as simply a business needing to compete among others, so that the last (action) hero of the university is neither the student nor the professor but the administrator. This apparent reorientation, however, necessarily sparks an anxiety concerning orientation itself, as the 'posthistorical', 'dereferentialised' university of excellence – now bereft of a content, reason, idea or even a (republican) promise – is exposed in new ways to the groundlessness of its grounding. (As we will see in Chapter 3 Readings is by no means simply pessimistic about this scenario.)

Bill Readings' work inspired the *Oxford Literary Review* 1995 special issue devoted to the question of the university as a ruined institution, and his own 'Dwelling in the ruins' was published here alongside essays by important critics such as J. Hillis Miller and Diane Elam. Concurrently, Peggy Kamuf's contribution to *Logomachia* was the first of several essays published by her during the 1990s, culminating in her book *The Division of Literature, Or, The University in Deconstruction*, appearing in 1997. Taking its bearings in a slightly different way to *The University in Ruins*, Kamuf's project is guided by a close analysis of the complex history of literary study in the modern university, particularly in Europe (especially France) and North America. Dealing with a wide variety of texts including those of the educational reformers of the French Revolution, the writings of Hippolyte Taine, Gustav Lanson and Charles Peguy, the fiction of Herman Melville and the public and journalistic discourse contributing to disputes over the canon and the PC wars of the last decade or so in the US, Kamuf's book reflects upon the question of the university as an institution by way of a reading of literary studies as a 'division' of the university: that is, as part of an institution that in important ways literary studies simultaneously partitions or describes.

This growing corpus of texts devoted to what seems a 'hot' topic in the 1990s would appear to establish the context for and justify, if not demand, further study. However, for reasons that I will come to later on I want, here, to stop short of developing a straightforward intellectual history regarding the renewal of academic interest in the question of the university as an institution. I also want, in the process, to refrain from simply re-presenting within a chronological trajectory the lineaments of a tradition that might seem to be reinvoked by a recent return to and rereading of (among others) Kant, Fichte, Schleiermacher, Schiller, Schelling, Humboldt, Newman, Arnold, Newbolt and also Hegel, Nietszche, Heidegger in terms of their role in the conceptualisation, founding and orientation of academic institutions. At various places in this book I will discuss more fully recent deconstructive studies of the university and thereby, inevitably, examine aspects of the university's intellectual traditions and genealogy. As I suggest in the conclusion, however, my concern will have been to attempt a different memory of the university, one that might evoke a temporality (for the institution) radically at odds with any suggestion of either simply a linear connection or a historicisable break between the 'founding fathers' of modern university education after Enlightenment and (destructive) 'posthistorical' deconstructionists – a temporality, indeed, radically at odds with any grandly comprehensive narrative of this sort. But, as I say, more on the question of history in a while.

My own project would of course be impossible without the body of work produced in recent times by these so-called deconstructionist critics (sometimes it has seemed impossible because of it!) and this book is therefore incalculably indebted to the authors and texts I refer to above. Nevertheless, I want not only to witness but in some way to countersign this work by returning to certain motifs and themes found in Derrida's work on orientation in the academic institution (a strange cluster that includes the lever or hinge, the idea of walking on two feet and the blinking of an eye, to name but a few) which, it seems to me, are increasingly overlooked or treated too hastily. By deploying these motifs I want in some sense to orient (disorient/reorient) a discussion of the relationship between recent academic debates in the humanities on the one hand, and the institutional setting of the university on the other. Therefore, the idea of leverage in particular not surprisingly provides the focus as well as the hinge for developing this discussion. And the questions which interest me throughout the book are these: if, as a number of critics now seem to agree, the university is in 'division' or 'ruin', not just now but from its very beginnings, then under such conditions how is leverage exerted within or around the institution? To what extent is this leverage fundamentally disoriented, an ongoing part of the university's ruins? Can leverage be exerted in such a way that disorientation need not simply be negatively marked?

In 'Mochlos' Derrida suggests that, just as the founding of the law is not a simply judicial question, one either of 'legality' or 'illegality', so the founding of the university cannot merely be treated as a 'university event'.[2] Rather, the founding of the university opens on to and is received from an otherness that everywhere permeates it. Thus the idea of the modern university as a unified institution with coherently defined characteristics and borders based from the outset on ideals of reason founders on its own foundations, and the university is beset by a conflict which 'is interminable and therefore insoluble' (p. 28). This conflict is one that can neither be attributed simply to an internal problematic – an avoidable glitch in the university's design arising as an oversight, if you like – nor easily dismissed as the result of intrusive, external intervention on the part of government or society. If, as Derrida therefore insists, 'there can be no pure concept of the university … due very simply to the fact that the university is *founded*' (pp. 29–30), in the face of this fundamental legitimation crisis he raises the question: how can we orient ourselves in (within, in relation to: the question already faces in more than one direction) the modern university?

Through a close reading of Kant's *The Conflict of the Faculties*, Derrida suggests that Kant attempts to contain and control the violently disruptive and divisive energies of this intractable crisis by insisting on its nature as mere 'conflict' as opposed to out-and-out 'war'. Thus, as Derrida puts it, Kant 'propos[es] for it a solution that is properly parliamentary' (p. 28). Here, the university is reconceived as a 'faculty parliament'. In this solution, the higher faculties (theology, law, medicine) occupy the right bench and defend the statutes of government, while the left bench is occupied by the philosophy faculty which offers 'rigorous examinations and objections' in the name and pursuit of truth. The opposition that results from this 'parliamentary solution' for Kant serves the higher purposes of a 'free system of government' and therefore resolves conflict into a more fundamental image of unity and accord. However, borrowing from Kant's 'What is orientation in thinking?',[3] Derrida and, in his essay 'The injured university',[4] Timothy Bahti, point out that 'right' and 'left' are not classified or recognised according to 'a conceptual or logical determination' but only from 'a sensory topology that has to be referred to the subjective position of the human body' (p. 31). This means that – as 'directions' – left and right cannot be fixed in universal terms according to incontrovertible logical determinants or objective principles governed and guided 'externally' by reason, so that the 'parliamentary' opposition between left and right into which the university's conflicts are projected and attemptedly resolved by Kant offer a no more reliable source of orientation for the university. As Bahti puts it, 'when we use corporeal directions we mean, "Be like me"' (p. 62), and therefore we address the other's right as if it were a left, the other's left as if it were a right. The resultant confusions between my left and another's right potentialised by this situation can be located not just in the subjective position of the human body, but in the sensory orientations collectively of parliamentary members within a body politic of modern, democratic, Western society developing after Kant. Thus, as Bahti points out with regard to certain modern institutions of government, 'in the parliamentary situation, the left – the "opposition" – is located from the perspective of the president or the speaker, but the speaker's left is obviously the left's right' (p. 62). The left from this point of view can only assert its leftness or oppositional stance by way of a (sensory or perceptual) repression of its right side. Indeed, paradoxically enough, its leftness and therefore its very oppositionality is only secured because the 'speaker or president', the overarching figure of authority in this situation, legitimates this reorientation, this repression, recasting right as left.

Such disorientations between left and right suggest an image of an unbalanced body, a body off-balance or suffering imbalance. A body, like the university, disoriented because it is unsure of its ground, its very foundations. In such a situation of imbalance, it is difficult to know how to proceed, what direction to take. Drawing on his own experience of undergoing therapy for a collapsed left lung, Bahti describes how, in order to restore balance, he was made by his physicians to adopt a position in which the weight of his body was by means of leverage shifted toward the healthy side (in this case, the right) 'inhibiting the free and strong use of the healthy lung, while forcing the injured side to do more of the breathing while it is also released of its "share" of the body's weight' (p. 68). This example of leverage, of levering between left and right, sets up a sort of dialogue with Derrida's essay 'Mochlos' (*mochlos* is a Greek word for lever). In 'Mochlos', it is the leverage between right and left, between inherited and newly founded laws, that in some way allows the body (the human body, the body politic, the body of the university) to walk, as it were, 'on two feet' (p. 31). Bahti is keen, however, to 'ward off a possible misunderstanding that might arise with the analogy of injury as imbalance', that is, the assumption that 'a certain symmetry, verging on stasis … is perhaps being held out as either an original health to be restored, or an ideal state to be attained, or both'. Rather, for Bahti, it is a question – especially when discussing the university – of 'recognizing imbalance as the condition within which leverage can and does take place' (pp. 73–4).

To put matters the other way round (as seems appropriate in the context of Bahti's comments about the parliamentary right and left), leverage – leverage within the university – is the condition of imbalance. This imbalance we have linked to an insoluble disorientation between left and right in a university uncertain as to its ground. All sorts of leverages that occur within the university (and which shape its institutions generally: its critical orthodoxies and counter-orthodoxies; its formations of disciplinary and interdisciplinary fields; its modes and discourse of publication, etc.) are, I would suggest, undertaken precisely by means of intractable confusions between left and right as, conventionally, sets of political meanings and values. Many have looked to these lefts and rights for orientation within the university; and many have attempted, on the basis of an identification of such 'fixed' positions, to exert leverage within the academic institution (in the language of the *Chambers Dictionary*, to impart pressure, to facilitate motion, to gain advantage or power 'over a resource greater than one actually owns': perhaps the university itself or, even beyond that, what(ever) founds it). I shall argue, however, that *dis*orientation is the condition, the starting point, of a leverage by which such orientation is sought. It is in a situation of *dis*orientation that orientation, direction, is attemptedly found (founded) through a mixture of constatives and performatives, statements and acts.

To take one example from among the case-study-ish analyses that make up this book: looking at some of the recurring themes and images arising in the early key texts of new historicism and cultural materialism, I argue in Chapter 2 that these approaches in a number of ways orient their critical strategies according to certain kinds of logics and structures of reflection. This orientation frequently takes the form either of an analysis of Renaissance power represented and discussed through a concentration on spectacle or, sometimes, painting, in which the mirror and the reflection, the 'glasse' and the 'eye', of power become the foremost tropes within new historicism's discursive formation (a mirror imagery with its own effects of power in which I argue new historicism itself becomes ensnared); or, as in the case of cultural materialism, through an assertion of the political relevance today of historical texts and events within which, as Robert Young puts it, 'cultural materialists re-assert a form of reflection theory, where history has become a mirror in which contemporary political priorities have been substituted for the former certain ground of Marxist analysis'[5] (i.e. substituted for dialectical materialism, in cruder forms of which history is less specular than linear). Both these emphases, these orientations, portray the object of their critical attention as a kind of mirror, then; and they seek to exert leverage within and against the institutions of criticism by means either of an analysis of power or an assertion of the possibilities of resistance, which equally depend on this mirror imagery. But, I argue, in so doing – indeed as a *condition* of so doing – they become *dis*oriented between left and right within the specular play of a struggle taking place 'through the looking glass' that none the less serves as the prerequisite for their critical orientations. Thus, in new historicism it is possible to see reflected the very formation and exercise of the kinds of power that new historicists wish to describe and expose. In cultural materialism, meanwhile, the attempt to dele-gitimise traditional or reactionary critical and political positions often depends on a strategy of demystification in which, paradoxi-cally, the dismantling of an imaginarily 'natural, obvious or right interpretation of an allegedly given textual fact'[6] (as Dollimore and Sinfield put it) frequently entails a formally symmetrical assertion of reference, truth and legality on the part of the politically radical critic. Sometimes, in fact, this even involves a commitment to, in one critic's phrase, 'objectivity and scholarship'[7] as a way of assert-ing difference from (right-wing) false politics; a commitment which nevertheless reproduces intact in the work of the politically radical (left-wing) critic the mystificatory stance of 'the *right* [my emphasis] interpretation of an allegedly given textual fact' that ironically establishes the impetus and rationale for its attack on the other. Here, the idea that leverage within the university depends on a per-sistent disorientation between left and right – and that direction, orientation, is established according to the imperative 'Be like me' which only compounds the confusion – has a profound resonance.

In Chapter 4, which takes its direction from issues thrown up by the multiple submissions debate in the US, I argue along similar lines that a kind of censorship existing institutionally as the 'very structure of the field' (Bourdieu) of academic discourse actually establishes the *possibility* of liberal discussion and radical critique of, for instance, the editorial policy of journals like *PMLA* during the 1990s, so that censorship from this perspective can be seen to have furnished the (impossible) conditions of possibility of enlightened academic expression. In this chapter, then, I undertake a critical examination of recent perspectives on censorship within contemporary Renaissance studies followed by a detailed reading of Bacon's vision of 'a college instituted for the interpreting of nature and the producing of great and marvellous works'[8] in *New Atlantis*, in order to suggest that such a disorientation between censorship, prohibition, regulation on the one hand and freedom, openness, enlightenment on the other might be regarded as a deep structure of the academy and its institutions. Bacon's text reveals the extent to which this disoriented interplay between apparent opposites somewhat ironically establishes the conditions under which academic orientation toward a future is itself attempted.

In a further section of the book, I discuss the problematical doubleness of economics as undecidably both inside and outside contemporary cultural theory. Here, I argue, the interdisciplinary approach of cultural criticism has a great deal of trouble positioning economics as either simply an outside – a prior discipline or an object of critical analysis – or an inside – in the form of the very structure of a system of exchange that interdisciplinarity seems to name or institute. Relatedly, within contemporary writing on 'culture', patterns of consumption can be identified as the categorised objects of authoritative critical representation, lending an empiral aura – by way of a certain critical distance – to semiotic and cultural analysis; but they can also be taken to structure academic desire itself which needs to consume in order to know. This disorientation between inside and outside I link to Derrida's discussion of the gift/*The Gift* as that which enables a shift (of nevertheless undecidable provenance) from 'cold economic rationality' to 'symbolicity' or '*total social fact*',[9] thereby 'founding' contemporary cultural discourse and interdisciplinary work in the humanities and human sciences generally. In this context, again, the orientation and leverage within the university seemingly offered by the development of cultural studies and by certain forms of interdisciplinarity comes at the expense of an insoluble disorientation between the activity and the object of criticism, whereby cultural analysis continually and undecidably affirms/negates its 'other', endlessly antagonising itself, doing itself violence.

Thus 'walking on two feet', to borrow the phrase Derrida uses to explore the issue of leverage, does not in any way create the impression of confident progress, concerted and coordinated movement forwards through concord or compromise between either 'side' or 'foot'. But neither does 'walking on two feet' (and how else could one walk?) simply present a comic picture of awkwardly self-conscious perambulation, to be ridiculed by those content in any case to stand still. More fundamentally, Derrida's image presents us with a potentially paralysing problem which nevertheless in some way we need to orient ourselves in relation to, whereby the impetus sought by one side or foot (left or right) depends wholly on the leverage received from the other. In the last section of my book I group together two essays, including the aforementioned consideration of economic and cultural discourse, under the heading 'Economies and exchanges'. Here I attempt to orient a discussion of the debates and dilemmas surrounding cultural studies, interdisciplinarity, and the 'survival' of critical and literary theory in the 1990s, by analysing the exchanges currently underway in the modern humanities via a consideration of the motifs of the gift and death found in various places in Derrida's work on the institution. In the last essay of the book, I discuss in a somewhat more polemical, affirmative way the implications and effects of deconstruction's survival on the discursive and institutional frontier constituted by debates about the 'life' and 'death' of (so-called) critical theory. Here, by paying close attention to Derrida's own work on death, I argue that the opposition between those that wish to preserve theory's 'life' and those that want to proclaim its 'death' (perhaps a discussion in which we find exerted the most leverage of all) is an impossibly constituted one. Yet I also argue that deconstruction's survival at the limit of coherence of this debate holds the promise for theory's future and, indeed, insistently puts the question of responsibility in the context of a modern interdisciplinary university whose exchanges (as the debate 'for' and 'against' deconstruction or theory shows) in fact exceed controlled regulation or final determination.

My arguments (concerning interdisciplinarity, for instance) therefore disorient somewhat the idea of disorientation as either a good or a bad thing. At times the emphasis of the book clearly falls on the unhelpful and counterproductive effects of certain kinds of disorientation in various debates regarding, for example, the politics of contemporary criticism, the orientation of cultural studies or the conditions of academic freedom in the current market of scholarly publication. Yet it is not my intention to suggest that this disorientation happens simply because some critics are stupid or confused in their work. Rather, in tune with Derrida's line of thought in essays such as 'Mochlos', 'The principle of reason' and 'Restitutions', the various discussions of disorientation and leverage found in this book depend implicitly on the notion that 'walking on two [undecidably left or right] feet' is in some way instituted as the very condition of academic life and thought. From this point of view there is within

the academy no secret enclave, no protected zone free from the taint
or trauma of disorientation, regardless of assertions to the contrary.
Indeed, as I point out in Chapter 4, the privileged role that Kant
envisaged for the philosophical faculty at Konigsberg entailed a
sturdy defence of academic freedom but nevertheless also imagined
philosophers as arbiters (effectively censors) of various forms of
knowledge produced by other faculty departments. If disorientation
establishes the conditions for the leverage exerted by academic work
of all kinds, then clearly it cannot merely be condemned as unequivocally a bad thing unless one seriously entertains the fantasy
of obliterating the university beyond all possible trace. Beyond all
possible trace: unless I have badly misread Derrida, deconstruction
is neither simply a matter of desiring nor of thinking possible the
obliteration of anything beyond all possible trace. So, it is not just a
question of disorientation (concerning direction, with regard to the
place of the boundary, and so forth) being either a good or a bad
thing. The question is rather how to receive, respond to, strategise,
capitalise on disorientation, how to view it, take steps within it,
speculate or bet on it, even how to survive it. What is at issue, then,
is 'living on' with a sort of deconstruction in and of the university
without simply flattening it out through overly glib assertions of the
reversibility of apparent (instituted) opposites, but instead taking
disorientation as an aporetic situation demanding response and
responsibility. While on occasion this book highlights some rather
disasterous examples of academic disorientation in recent times, and
perhaps even more depressingly (for some) presents disorientation
as longstanding and self-reproducing rather than symptomatic of
a sudden crisis or moment of breakdown, it therefore also represents
an attempt to stay with and think through the problem in its various guises, in order not just to negate but also affirm the possibilities of academic effort.

Some of what follows may at first glance seem rather strange.
Why would anyone want to explore problems facing the university
by way of a long first chapter on Van Gogh's shoes, for example?
Aside from the fact that Derrida's comments towards the end of
'Mochlos' seem to lead us along that route, surely it would be better to disregard such fanciful endeavours in favour of an empirical
account either of the economic, political and ideological pressures

encountered by today's universities or, at least, an explanation along more familiar historical lines of intellectual trends and developments that may have contributed to the current situation (even the recent analyses) of the institution. Such approaches seem pressing, not to say urgent, and in any case we might think they were possessed of more obvious explanatory power. Indeed, I would not pretend to dispense with them entirely. Clearly the explorations of new historicism, cultural studies, interdisciplinarity and theory's 'survival' I offer here seem to predicate a wider situation of some historical moment or significance, raising questions of the temporal dimension of the institution's problems that in different ways I try to attend to at various times in the book. Equally it is clear that recent deconstructive writing on the university, with which this project engages, quite frequently presents itself as not altogether incompatible with the narrative strategies of an historical account. The books by Readings and Kamuf, discussed more extensively in Chapter 3, are obvious examples here, although significantly in the work of both these critics the presentation of history is mediated, inflected and to some extent challenged by rather rigorous critical reflection on the question of the institution's temporality which, at times, appears fundamentally out of step with historical exegesis in its cruder forms. This is partly the reason why a straightforward historical approach of the kind that would seem most useful or pressing, installing itself as a stabilising context or background in terms of which each chapter might be read and viewed as a particular stage or expression of a period-based, chronologically driven argument, does not finally preoccupy or determine the 'deconstructive' analyses offered here. However let us once again leave aside, for the moment at least, the broader question of deconstruction's relation to history. It is one that we will look at in Chapter 3 and also more fully in the conclusion, where I attempt to re-collect the various analyses undertaken in this book in terms of an art of memory quite incompatible with the 'historical' in its conventional sense. For the time being I would just like to hint at reasons for my reluctance, overall, to indulge in any kind of conventional history as a way to flesh out the particular project I have envisaged.

Just as it would be absurd and self-contradictory to try to account for the institutional disorientation of paired opposites such as left and right, academic freedom and institutional censorship, theory's life and death, etc. by way of splitting disorientation into neatly opposed 'good' and 'bad' forms, so it would surely be unadvisable to present the case concerning disorientation by charting in more orthodox ways a predominating history that is felt to be behind the problem. How, without devastating irony, could one (re)orient a book on disorientation by developing a periodising argument following, quite complacently, the linear trajectory plotted by less complex forms of economic, sociopolitical or intellectual history? If I am arguing (and seeking to demonstrate through a variety of readings and texts) that disorientation is the condition of academic life, thought and work, how would it be possible to find a position from which to place with any confidence the history *behind* the situation? In any case, the kind of history that might be demanded in place of a chapter on Van Gogh's shoes – the kind that seems urgent and replete with explanatory force – would, in its useful or end-oriented form, doubtless aim to exert some sort of leverage in the university. If, as I argue, leverage can only take place in a situation of imbalance arising from the disorientation experienced by an institution unsure of its ground, then logically speaking an (end-)oriented history exerting leverage in the form of usefulness would arise only as a condition of disorientation. In other words, a straightforward historical description might try to conceal or repress its own disorientation but could never escape (because of) its confused directionality.

Hence, while in different ways according to the specificity of the analysis I locate the conditions of historicity or temporality within the problems of disorientation and leverage, my account of uncoordinated movements within the university cannot in the last instance be determined according to, as it were, the objective co-ordinates or reliable accounts supplied by a normative, overarching or teleological history. Instead of trying to frame my analyses in terms of a past reconstructed in very familiar ways, I aim merely to underscore, as Peggy Kamuf says of her own work on the university, 'certain conceptual negotiations with the distinctions that would define this new institution',[10] the institution of the modern academic establishment. Does this mean, however, that the project is inevitably divested of end-oriented or useful purpose? Is the chapter on Van Gogh's shoes condemned to be read and discarded as just metaphorical because of the avowed impossibility of reference or literalism? Should the book really and truthfully be called *Disorientation in the University, Figuratively Speaking*? Or perhaps, really and truthfully, *Leverage in the University, Figuratively Speaking*?

Setting aside the contradiction already implicit in this question, I want to suggest that leverage cannot simply be shrugged off as just another metaphor demanding translation, interpretation or application for it to be useful. A lever is a tool or structure, one part or point of which is fixed while another exerts force against a body by utilising the pressure of that which resists it. On this definition, far from presenting itself as just another figurative device, the lever itself establishes the very conditions of metaphor. In a recent interview, discussed in more detail in Chapter 6, Derrida argues that to 'relate to an object *as such* means to relate to it as if you were dead'.[11] The outcome of this impossible wish to grasp the truth or objectivity of an object is that the *as such* becomes shot through with the *as if*. The *as if* is therefore the supplement, the inexhaustible and incalculable remainder, that just cannot be left out or cashed out of the *as such*. Through its remorseless and unstinting *play* with the literal or referential, then, the analogical or figural cannot in the usual manner be thought simply to illuminate that which exists, literally, outside itself. Rather, the analogue offers an intralinguistic deixis or indication which, as Giorgio Agamben notes, 'does not simply demonstrate an unnamed object, but above all the very instance of discourse, its taking place'.[12] In an elementary way, analogies, figures, metaphors might thus be thought to be different from 'conventional' language, i.e. in its representational normativity. Yet, as Derrida demonstrates, they remain everywhere embedded in it as an essential and unavoidable feature of language itself: the *as if* is always the upshot of the *as such*. As *if* thus survives as the irreducible supplement of language – that is, in an originary 'relation' to it. The metaphor hinges on a fixed point (a reference point) only to exert force against the body which resists it (referential language) by means of that body's own pressure.

In other words, leverage is not just a metaphor, but metaphor is (literally) a lever. From this point of view, it is inaccurate to say that this book on leverage merely speaks figuratively of the university;

although it now becomes possible to see how, despite the apparent lack of end-oriented or conventionally useful purpose, the project might exert leverage. I want to begin therefore by following the footsteps that lead from 'Mochlos' to Van Gogh's shoes, and from there to the question of the institution and of institutionality, before travelling anew any of the more familiar paths that might guide us to the near or distant histories of the university.

Notes

1 Bill Readings, *The University in Ruins* (Cambridge, Mass., and London: Harvard University Press, 1996), p. 15. All further references will be given in the main body of the text.

2 Jacques Derrida, 'Mochlos', in *Logomachia: The Conflict of the Faculties*, ed. Richard Rand (Lincoln, NB and London: University of Nebraska Press, 1992), pp. 28–9. All further references will be given in the main body of the text.

3 Immanuel Kant, 'What is orientation in thinking?', in *Political Writings* 2nd edition, ed. Hans Reiss (Cambridge: Cambridge University Press, 1992). The emphasis on disorientation with regard to Kant in this section of my essay may appear to do him an injustice. Howard Caygill in *Art of Judgement* (Oxford: Basil Blackwell, 1989) draws attention to ways in which Kant attempts to (re)orient thinking in light of the problem of orientation. It is not my concern here to follow in detail the complexity of Kantian thought on this subject or evaluate the headway Kant makes with regard to it. I want simply to draw attention, as Derrida does, to the primary difficulty of establishing orientation according to the 'sensory topology' of left and right not only in general terms but specifically within the university.

4 Timothy Bahti, 'The injured university', in *Logomachia*, ed. Richard Rand. All further references will be given in the main body of the text.

5 Robert Young, *White Mythologies: Writing History and the West* (London: Routledge, 1990), p. 89.

6 Jonathan Dollimore and Alan Sinfield, 'Foreword', in *Political Shakespeare: New Essays in Cultural Materialism*, ed. Jonathan Dollimore and Alan Sinfield (Manchester: Manchester University Press, 1985), p. viii.

7 Walter Cohen, 'Political criticism of Shakespeare', in *Shakespeare Reproduced: The Text in History and Ideology*, ed. Jean Howard and Marion O' Connor (London: Methuen, 1987), p. 20.

8 Francis Bacon, *New Atlantis and The Great Instauration*, ed. Jerry Weinberger (Illinois: Harlan Davidson, 1989), p. 36.

9 See Jacques Derrida's studies of Mauss's *The Gift*, 'The time of the king' and 'The madness of economic reason', in his *Given Time: 1. Counterfeit Money*, trans. Peggy Kamuf (Chicago, IL and London: University of Chicago Press, 1992), pp. 1–33; pp. 34–70.

10 Peggy Kamuf, *The Division of Literature, Or, The University in Deconstruction* (Chicago, IL: University of Chicago Press, 1997), p. 75.

11 Jacques Derrida, '*As if* I were dead: an interview with Jacques Derrida', in *Applying: To Derrida*, ed. John Brannigan, Ruth Robbins and Julian Wolfreys (London: Macmillan, 1996), p. 216.

12 Georgio Agamben, *Language and Death: The Place of Negativity*, trans. Karen E. Pinkus and Michael Hardt (Minneapolis, MN: University of Minnesota Press, 1991), quoted in Ronald Schleifer, 'Afterword: Walter Benjamin and the crisis of representation: multiplicity, meaning, and athematic death', in *Death and Representation*, ed. Sarah Webster Goodwin and Elisabeth Bronfen (Baltimore, MD and London: The Johns Hopkins University Press, 1993), p. 321.

PART 1

Authorities

CHAPTER 1

Van Gogh's shoes, or, does the university have two left feet?

as Kant will have told us, the university will have to go on two feet, left and right, each foot having to support the other as it rises with each step to make the leap. It involves walking on two feet, two feet *with shoes*, since it turns on an institution, on a society and a culture, not just on nature. This was already clear in what I recalled about the faculty parliament. But I find its confirmation in an entirely different context, and you will certainly want to forgive me this rather rapid and brutal leap; I am authorized by the memory of a discussion, held in this very place some two years ago with our eminent colleague, Professor Meyer Shapiro, on the subject of certain shoes in Van Gogh.

Jacques Derrida, 'Mochlos'[1]

Foot fetishism

On the basis of my introductory discussion of disorientation and leverage in the university, negotiated through Derrida's image of 'walking on two feet', I propose in this first chapter to consider a number of instances of (for want of a better term) foot fetishism[2] as they arise in twentieth-century critical thought, many of which seem to offer a way for thinkers to gain a sort of foothold, to attempt or explore orientation in their respective fields. Examples will include: Heidegger's analysis in his essay 'The origin of the work of art' of Van Gogh's depiction of shoes; Frederic Jameson's discussion in 'The cultural logic of late capitalism' of portrayals of footwear in modern

art, where Van Gogh's painting and Heidegger's analysis importantly receive mention; and Derrida's own encounter with Van
Gogh's painting of shoes, via the correspondence between Heidegger
and Shapiro, in 'Restitutions'. In levering between such texts, then,
it may well be possible to trace some of the key philosophical and
theoretical orientations of late modernity in the context of the
humanities and human sciences. Without wanting to present grand
claims concerning twentieth-century intellectual history, however, I
will suggest that the critical issue raised by Van Gogh's painting –
whether the shoes are properly a pair or whether they are not a pair
at all, paradoxically because they may be the same – is important in
terms of a number of critical procedures and, more widely, opens on
to the question of the academic institution itself. The problem of
Van Gogh's painting is one that might very well help guide us
(although only on the basis of a disoriented figure of two
paired/unpaired shoes or feet) through at least some of the debates
surrounding, for example, Marxism, poststructuralism, postmodernism and deconstruction within the university. Aside from the
familiar sort of intellectual and methodological disputes we find
here, however, it is my concern to ask: does the university as an institution itself stand in a specular relation, a relation of reflection, to
Van Gogh's painting of shoes? Taking direction from the painting, in
terms of the address: 'Be like me', does the university itself have two
left feet? Let us take a few steps towards or, more precisely, within
this question.

Step one: Jameson's 'The cultural logic of late capitalism'

Jameson's attempt to delineate the constitutive features of the postmodern according to a periodising logic – that of late capitalism
in the latter half of the twentieth century, whereby 'aesthetic
production today has become integrated into commodity production generally' – is elucidated by way of a comparative analysis of
portrayals of footwear in late nineteenth- and twentieth-century
art.[3] Jameson finds in Van Gogh's peasant shoes ('one of the canonical works of high modernism' (p. 6)) a vibrant, organic immediacy,
the painting itself gloriously transforming the poverty, abjection and
oppression that it takes as its subject within a 'Utopian realm of the

senses'. This artisic realm thus constitutes itself as 'semiautonomous space', 'a part of some new division of labour in the body of capital', one that not simply replicates capitalism's tendency toward specialisation but which enables Utopian dreams to emerge out of the fragmenting pressures of the modern world (pp. 6–7). Here, as we shall see, Jameson is closer to Shapiro than Heidegger in identifying the painting at bottom with the rhythms of 'the city dweller' instead of 'the peasant' in an age of 'industrial technology' rather than 'artisanal production', as Derrida has put it.[4] However, drawing also on Heidegger's analysis, Jameson insists on the hermeneutical value of Van Gogh's painting of shoes. By this he means that 'the work in its inert, objectal form is taken as a clue or a symptom for some vaster reality which replaces it as its ultimate truth' (p. 8). (It is disputable whether these are the appropriate terms with which to describe Heidegger's 'The origin of the work of art', or whether its analysis is 'hermeneutical' in the sense proposed by Jameson: see below.) All this is contrasted with the phoney glamour, the glitzy flatness or depthlessness, the deathly whiff of simulacra, the hermeneutic emptiness and sense of political inertia that (supposedly) surrounds Warhol's study of mass-produced, commodity-fetishised footwear in *Diamond Dust Shoes*.

Yet this analysis is somewhat compressed, to put it mildly. By his own admission Jameson embarks upon a comparison between Van Gogh's painting of a pair of peasant shoes and Warhol's *Diamond Dust Shoes* as a means to demonstrate the vast shift between high modernism and postmodernism, yet he devotes only four pages of this lengthy essay to the two works (during which he also manages to fit in a quick word on the treatment of footwear in Magritte and Walker Evans) before swiftly moving on to pick up the theme of the 'waning of human affect' (p. 10) this century with reference to pop art icons and to Munch's *The Scream*. It is as if we are being hurried through a virtual gallery of art works (in *Postmodernism* glossy reproductions in colour are interspersed with text, and indeed take up about as much page space as the analysis of them). Jameson treats us to the easily digestible and reproducible view offered by the tour guide, where critical insights are exchanged in the form of commodifiable information (the sound bite). Here we have all the elements of the postmodern as described by Jameson himself: simulacrum and the 'deep constitutive relationships of ... a whole new technology' (the glossy reproductions); depthlessness (the superficiality of Jameson's 'scratch the surface and all will be revealed', non-contemplative approach); a 'weakening of historicity' in light of the compacted and compressed attention span that situates Jameson's essay within commodified postmodern time, and so forth (p. 6). Furthermore, by rushing us past great works according to a kind of viewing that conforms to all the constitutive dimensions and technics of the postmodern, the essay offers itself in or indeed *as* a space that virtually simulates the giddying hyperspace of late twentieth-century architecture: 'Here the narrative stroll has been ... replaced by a transportation machine', the escalator, the elevator, the conveyor-belt (p. 42).

While such remarks seem to fit well with my general argument concerning disorientation in contemporary criticism, I make these observations about the critical practice of 'The cultural logic of late capitalism' not simply to suggest that Jameson ironically and unwittingly reproduces in the space of his essay all the features of the postmodern that he seems otherwise to lament or regret. Actually I wish to point out something else more profoundly ill-fitting about this piece of work. That is, this: it is difficult to see how shoes can fit here as that which might lead us toward the meaning of the shift from high modernism to postmodernism, when shoes themselves now stand (or, rather than being hung on a gallery wall, are more radically suspended in their technologically simulated, glossily reproduced forms) in a space which, beyond requiring us to walk *impossibly* quickly, introduces hyperspatial-cyberspatial possibilities that in fact sound the death-knell of walking itself. If Jameson were to extend further his analysis of commodity fetishism, hermeneutic emptiness and spiritless death in Warhol's *Diamond Dust Shoes* to suggest that footwear in postmodernism is on the verge of becoming not just devoid of deeper meaning but actually, fundamentally obsolete (as footwear is virtually obsolete in the postmodern space of Jameson's essay gallery) then there might once more be a fit in 'The cultural logic of late capitalism' between the diagnosis of the postmodern and the choice of figure used to illustrate this, between the substantive content of the essay and its critical practice. Or so one might think. However, the irony here would not only be that footwear must remain, in an ill-fitting way, necessary to highlight its own obsolence, but that the development of such insights would require the analysis to be further extended, to change its stride, to lengthen its journey and, as it were, moderate its pace. In other words, in order to proclaim the radical obsolesence of footwear we (along with Jameson) would have to take ourselves out of the 'transportation machine' and return paradoxically to something like the 'narrative stroll'. To see that shoes are altogether done away with, to stop them being ill-fitting, we would, in an altogether ill-fitting way, have to put them back on.

All this is to suggest that the shoes which Jameson takes to lead us toward the postmodern are radically out of joint with the time and space of the postmodernism he describes. It is not so much that they walk in an entirely opposite direction but that, by disappearing within the postmodern as the figure which nevertheless best locates it, and by fully exemplifying postmodernism's inner workings only by stepping outside it, they utterly disorient the direction which Jameson takes, or thinks he takes, toward the postmodern itself (which in any case, for Jameson as a Marxist critic of late capitalism, is in some sense also a direction *against* the postmodern). Devoid of hermeneutic value or depth of meaning, shoes for Jameson may well have lost the capacity to fulfil Enlightenment dreams of forward motion, of linear progress towards a Utopian goal; and they may now for him seem compelled to tread the ceaselessly circular paths of postmodern intertextuality, simulacra, late capitalist consumption and political inertia. But by way of a closer look at Jameson's essay we find that shoes retain or reserve a radical alterity here, in that they only ever step inside the circle of postmodernism in the form of stepping outside it.

How can we account for the double bind of shoes as an 'accessory' in the case of Jameson? Let us take another step, a detour perhaps en route to (or, again, within) the question with which we began.

Step two: Heidegger's 'The origin of the work of art'

In philosphical terms the import of Heidegger's 'The origin of the work of art' has to do with his notion that earth and world – more usually understood as matter and content – find a unity which arises out of conflict: this Heidegger calls the '*Riss*', an almost untranslatable term which carries a sense both of rift and design.[5] For Heidegger, the strife that arises from the opposition between material and content simultaneously furnishes the design by which, as Hofstadter and Kuhns put it, 'content is actualized in the material' (p. 648). Thus it is that the truth of Being reveals itself in art since this unity born of strife (*Riss*) is set to work and stands in the art work. Heidegger's larger philosophical claims about the origin and nature of works of art are illustrated (although as Derrida suggests this may not be the best way to describe Heidegger's 'example') by a discussion of Van Gogh's painting. This serves, neatly enough, as the equipment for his argument that equipmental beings – such as a pair of peasant shoes – by ocupying an intermediate place between the thing and the work in fact help us comprehend 'things and works and ultimately everything that is' (p. 660), thus establishing the context in which Heidegger's reflections on earth, world, *Riss* and the revelation of the truth of Being can themselves stand or be set forth. Instead of placing the accent on these wider philosophical questions that, by and large, come into view once Heidegger has dealt with the painting by Van Gogh, I will concentrate here on the first part of his essay leading up to the discussion of the peasant shoes. I do so in order to explore how, as equipment, shoes equip Heidegger to develop, in Hofstadter and Kuhns' terms, 'a new and suggestive approach to the concrete work of art'(p. 649); one which, by compelling itself to 'follow the circle' (p. 651) traced out by certain impassable problems in the conceptual machinery of traditional aesthetics, in some respect passes beyond them, indeed passing (opening) on to the question that concerns us.

Heidegger's essay begins by raising the question of the origin of the work of art in terms of the source of its essence or nature. The commonplace view that the art work 'arises out of and by means of the activity of the artist' is quickly subjected to a logical reversal in that, simultaneously for Heidegger, it is possible to say that the artist arises out of the work; that it 'does credit to the master' and thus by means of itself 'lets the artist emerge' (p. 650). Within the origination of art, therefore, artist and work seem endlessly to replace one another as source, appearing mutually dependent since, 'Neither is without the other'. Yet, according to Heidegger, it is not simply the case that the artist and the work are just two legs, as it were, bound to one another in a relation of somewhat antagonistic dependency, a relation of both friction and leverage, ungoverned or uncoordinated by any third term and hence left to go around in circles. Heidegger tells us that 'neither is the sole support of the other', but that each is produced ('named') and regulated 'by virtue of a third thing which is prior to both' – art itself. Yet, in immediate terms at least, art proves a no more reliable source of orientation towards the origin of art. Heidegger is quick to recognise that art is rather slippery and intangible. As a word or term it passes foremost 'for a collective idea under which we find a place for that which alone is real in art: works and artists'. In other words, the idea of art manifests itself only to describe what manifests *it*, i.e. the rather more tangible 'actuality' of the various artists and art works that are grouped together in the name of 'art' but which art is nevertheless thought to pre-exist. In this way, art can only ever be used to describe itself in the same way that a compass is used to describe a circle. Bound within the self-same pattern of reversible relations it was introduced to overrule, rather than curbing reversibility according to the orderly logic of a stable third term, art itself confirms such relations as an interminable series.

However, Heidegger seems unwilling so early in his essay to give himself over negatively to this problem as an impassable dilemma. Instead, he continues to insist that art, the nature of art (which is inextricably linked to the question of its origins), 'should be inferable from the work' as 'the place where art undoubtedly prevails in a real way' (p. 650). This assertion is based in large measure on a refusal to follow the tendency in Enlightenment thought to seek 'derivation from higher concepts' (p. 651). Yet it is made despite the fact that, as Heidegger knows only too well, any kind of empirical or comparative method – as the other 'leg' that orients or levers Enlightenment thinking – always constitutes a problematic closure on the question of the nature of art or indeed the truth of Being which it reveals. Heidegger is himself in a double bind, therefore; one which suggests itself as the counterpart to the twinship and reversibility of artist and work and indeed the circularity of art itself. On the one hand, he wants to deconstruct – in the very question of the origin of the work of art – the empirico-transcendental difference of Enlightenment thought, but on the other hand it seems that any such deconstruction remains bound within the limits and effects of the kinds of circularity such thought institutes.

Or, as seems entirely appropriate, to reverse this formulation: any deconstruction of the circle-effects produced by and producing 'the usual view', 'ordinary understanding' or 'logic' (as Heidegger variously puts it) – something that begins to happen here in the very question of the origin of the work of art – requires one to move resolutely *within* the circle. Thus Heidegger can affirm 'we are compelled to follow the circle ... Not only is the main step from work to art a circle like the step from art to work, but every separate step that we attempt circles in this circle' (p. 651). Here, paradoxically, the 'step' forwards takes a turn, turns on itself, in a circle. It is as if, by remaining within the circle, Heidegger can lay bare the manifestations of circularity that everywhere attend the linear idea of progress in thinking that characterises vulgar thought. This indeed establishes the conditions for the Heideggerian 'step', as a kind of earlier version of Derrida's idea of 'walking on two feet', where the lever that propels one forward nevertheless roots itself to the spot where one is to achieve this, thus demanding a radical rethinking of 'newness' or invention.

It is perhaps no surprise, then, that in order to keep open the question, to infer art from the work, Heidegger turns to Van Gogh's painting of a pair of shoes. The painting initially crops up in the discussion alongside a number of remarks concerning the 'actuality' or thingly character of works of art. The first thing that Heidegger wants to say about a painting such as 'the one by Van Gogh that represents a pair of peasant shoes' is that it 'travels from one exhibition to another' (p. 651). Works are bound within the 'actuality' of exchanges and events happening in everyday time and publicly constituted space, and from this point of view they are treated no differently than other 'objects': 'Works are shipped like coal from the Ruhr and logs from the Black Forest'. However, one would have to grossly underestimate Heidegger's guile – and indeed the critical procedure that unfolds in this essay – to suggest that the choice of Van Gogh's painting as a first example occurs as mere coincidence. The contiguous, associative, 'two way' relation between the inside and outside of the painting, between the pair of shoes in the picture and the 'travel' it undergoes in its actual or thingly capacity, suggests that we are not dealing merely with one 'thing' among others, or one instance of a generality (and therefore not merely with an example, as Derrida in various ways demonstrates: we will come back to this). Instead, Heidegger's choice of Van Gogh's painting, as supposedly an illustration or proof within his discussion, (un)cannily reactivates the series of reversible relations that mark out the circle in which his essay needs to move in order to keep open (rather than too hastily close off, resolve, decide upon) the question of the origin and nature of the work of art.

Thus, all of Heidegger's preliminary difficulties in ascribing origins in view of the question of art are reinvoked by way of this (so-called) example. According to its thingly quality, does Van Gogh's painting of a pair of shoes simply remain bound within a nexus of 'actuality' which paralyses it as a work of art, now no different to any other banal 'thing'? Or, in the case of a painting of a pair of shoes that is made to travel – and I choose the word 'made' deliberately here, since for Heidegger 'madeness' is an important feature of works of art and here might therefore suggest fitness for the purpose as much as the application of force – is it rather that the art work itself gets up and walks before any such moment of bondage or paralysis? Certainly the painting seems to exist in a dimension of time that places it somewhat beyond the moment when Heidegger himself, through exercising the force of his critical faculties, attributes a thingly quality to it. Or, to be more exact, it is precisely in the process of apparently presenting Van Gogh's picture as an initial example that Heidegger (rather cannily, I would suggest) reveals that its origins must lie beyond this first move or instance, this apparent beginning. Thus, the first thing Heidegger has to say about the painting he seems to choose as a guiding illustration proves (somewhat knowingly) to be no 'first thing' at all, since the painting – as one of a pair of shoes that 'travels' – is already in transit, already coming from elsewhere.

Yet this transit, which places the art work just beyond one's reach or grasp as a tangible object of knowledge, is made possible *only because of* its thingly character, its madeness or fitness for the purpose. Thus, 'a piece of equipment, a pair of shoes for instance' would be what sets the painting on the road toward art, since in Heidegger's terms, 'Equipment has a peculiar position intermediate between thing and work' (pp. 659–60). Hence, Heidegger tells us, 'even the much-vaunted aesthetic experience cannot get around the thingly aspect of the art work'; although it is worth noting once again the paradox that this thingliness also places works of art beyond any vulgar conception of the thingly, as Heidegger's 'example' itself demonstrates. Here, we are at once 'compelled to follow the circle' and by following it able to take a certain 'step' with regard to deconstructing the empirico-transcendental difference of much Enlightenment thought. The same effect occurs where Heidegger ponders the idea that something other than *techne* or madeness enters into the nature of the art work, something we call allegory or symbol; but that symbol ('in Greek, *sumballein*') can be seen as nothing other than the name for a bringing together, the making of a join, that is itself 'the thingly feature in the art work' (p. 652). Similarly, when Heidegger asks, 'Is the structure of a simple propositional statement (the combination of subject and predicate) the mirror image of the structure of the thing (of the union of substance with accidents)?' (p. 655) – a question he qualifies at length and ultimately leaves unresolved – the relations between language and materiality, subject and object, are once more encountered within an interminably reversible or at least spectrally undecidable trajectory of thought which disrupts the possibility of straightforward logical progression or any conventional attribution of origins that might accompany an 'ordinary' or 'usual' treatise on, in this case, the issue of what a thing *is*. Thus, once more it would seem that in order to take any kind of 'step', Heidegger's essay has, like Van Gogh's painting, to 'walk on two feet', to remain in the circle that encircles subject and object, materiality and language, words and things, matter and form, movement and stasis.

The distinction between matter and form is in fact presented by Heidegger as of longstanding and crucial importance 'in the domain in which we are supposed to be moving' (p. 658). He identifies this distinction as the basis for *the conceptual schema which is used, in the greatest variety of ways, quite generally for all art theory and aesthetics*. When this distinction between form and matter is correlated with the oppositional pairings of the rational and irrational and of subject and object, a conceptual machinery is put in place 'that nothing is capable of withstanding'. In the face of this recognition, Heidegger wants to 'make use of' rather than simply reject as obselete or worn-out the distinction between matter and form. He wants to 'recover its defining power' (p. 659), to reinhabit its madeness in order to recommence his journey with respect to the question of art's nature. In other words, he wants to renew the matter-form structure as equipment, indeed as something like a pair of shoes with which one could 'walk on two feet', step within the circle, exert leverage by utilising a certain rootedness to the spot. On this view, the matter-form structure itself enters into the interminable series of reversibilities that encircle the question of art itself, and the dilemma that for Heidegger surrounds the question of the origins of this structure (whether it comes, as it were, from the subject or the object, materiality or representation, from the 'thingly character of the thing' or 'the workly character of the art work') places it within the self-same circle. Only now, of course, the issue is even more undecidable (if that were possible) since the matter-form distinction is inextricably always already made up of these oppositional pairings that one cannot therefore decide between.

Hence the *relationship* between form and matter which in some way for Heidegger seems to enter into, even define, the thingly element – in turn opening on to the question of the nature or origin of art – is itself originally and originarily reversible. It is not simply the case, for example, that matter pre-exists form since the distribution of matter is determined by form. The 'interfusion of form and matter' is in fact determined by the 'purposes served by jug, ax, shoes', to quote Heidegger's 'examples' (p. 659). In other words, form and matter interlock because of purpose. This nevertheless seems a rather fragile third term in that, entailing the idea of design, it appears to incline purpose towards form, if not fold it back into form altogether and thereby establish a certain priority over matter. Yet purpose or usefulness 'is never assigned or added on afterwards to ... a jug, ax, or a pair of shoes'. If purpose cannot stand above or outside the thing itself as its 'end', then neither does it simply fold back into its form to establish form as the ultimate destination of matter. This is because purpose (as a species of form) occurs simultaneously with matter in the character of the thing, and does not merely come after it. The decision as to what a 'jug, ax, or a pair of shoes' are *for* does not occur *after* they are made, so that madeness cannot be thought simply in terms of the eventual triumph of form over matter. To some extent, this *fort/da* returns us to the example of an art work itself, where the concept or form of a symbol or allegory in art – as that which is imagined to lift art above the merely thingly – actually entails joining, madeness, which is in fact the very characteristic of the thing. For Heidegger, then, a jug, an ax, or a pair of shoes cannot be made without an idea of what they are for, yet this idea cannot form itself beforehand or without the element and quality of matter: that is, 'impermeable for a jug, sufficiently hard for an ax, firm yet flexible for shoes'.

This last quality – of shoes – turns on a paradox (and not only because it combines in the character of the thing the 'firm' with the 'flexible', although needless to say this would bring us back once again to the idea of leverage). Shoes are fashioned, made, turned upon a last. This seems to capture a certain tension between, on the one hand, a sense of finality, finitude, finishedness (the product of the 'last') and, on the other, ongoingness, impermanence, flux, work ('turning'). Yet of course 'turning' and the 'last' are utterly coterminous and mutually dependent in the process of making. Hence, 'A piece of equipment, a pair of shoes for instance, when finished, is also self-contained like the mere thing, but it does not have the character of having taken shape by itself' (pp. 659–60). Here an odd supplementarity (madeness itself?) installs itself in the character of the thingly, in the form of the contradictory and unresolvable division between the making of the shoes (they do not take shape by themselves, even when finished) and the shoes as made (although 'finished' and 'self-contained', their character is not exactly their own but the product of an other). This renders them, at one and the same time, both self-same and other and (therefore) neither self-same nor wholly other. But perhaps this is not after all surprising when we recall that the equipment under discussion is shoes, which always display the curious quality of being a 'proper' pair by virtue of their difference. Any two shoes that were to attain 'self-sameness' in the sense of being identical to one another would, however paradoxical it may seem, not be a pair at all. They would certainly not function 'properly' as equipment. One could not easily walk with them. But this is to suggest something quite shocking about equipment, be it technical or, indeed, theoretical, since we have detected in Heidegger's analysis not only a contemplation of thing, equipment, work, art, etc. but also, for want of a better term, a discourse on method (although of course the division or distinction between the two greatly offends everything that is going on in this essay). Heidegger's pointedly chosen 'example' of shoes in his discussion of the origin of works of art alerts us to the possibility that the only kind of equipment that might really be useful depends on a supplementarity which everywhere reverses reasoned distinctions and thus suspends logical progression – yet one would think that a basic level of distinguishability between opposites (between right and left) leading to the possibility of forward movement (in the ordinary sense of walking) was fundamental to the very purpose and nature of shoes as equipment! The usefulness of a pair of shoes as a type of equipment therefore depends bizarrely upon processes of making and employment that – when scrutinised along the lines of Heidegger's essay – would seem to go against what, at the most basic level, we would imagine they were *for*. Here in a certain way we are going (stepping) back to everything we said about Jameson.

From this point of view, it is not just the case that shoes (if they function at all) will simply lead us to walk (in) the wrong way or take the opposite direction from the one we really wanted. More fundamentally, by going *against* what they are *for*, shoes as equipment will always lead to a certain disorientation of direction itself: a step within a circle. (Heidegger begins his analysis 'proper' of Van Gogh's painting, appropriately enough in mid-essay, by declaring 'we cannot even tell where these shoes stand' (p. 663).) Of course, if we continue to take the shoes as akin to theoretical equipment, there are times when this disorientation between what one is *for* and what one is *against* has proved quite disasterous for certain modes of knowing, certain critical discourses and practices, and certainly certain sorts of politics within the university. My earlier comments on cultural materialism (developed more fully in the next chapter) suggest as much. Such calamitous disorientations often occur when difficulties and dilemmas of the kind we have been discussing lead people to, as Heidegger puts it, 'disavow thought instead of making it more thoughtful' (p. 656). Not surprisingly, amidst all the confusion between for and against, any such escape route will inevitably lead straight back to the heart of the problem. Under the guise of an appeal to finally determinable solutions or ways out, such tunnels are dug by people who in actual fact want to give up, turn back, rather than push on. However, disorientation need not always be marked negatively in this way. It is just that, when disorientation proves to be a bad or unhelpful thing, it is usually because the equipment is not being used properly – which is to say that, paradoxically, a kind of *improper* use must be observed and respected if one is to get anywhere. The lesson Heidegger teaches us is that the use of shoes is always improper, since they are actually *against* what they are *for*. Yet by using shoes according to their proper improper use, Heidegger is himself able to take a 'step'. Shoes as equipment occupy a 'peculiar' intermediate position between 'thing and work', but it is precisely because they are, properly speaking, improper, paradoxical, monstrous, hybrid, uncanny, neither this nor that, that they equip or help us to reflect on the no more proper or pure origins of the thing and the work: 'things and works and ultimately everything that is – are to be comprehended with the help of the being of equipment' (p. 660). In an interminable process of transit among a ceaseless series of reversible relations within the circle, equipment always carries with it an odd sense of the conjunction of stasis and movement we find here. And of course it is such a conjunction between stasis and movement that furnishes the conditions of possibility for the very idea of leverage.

Perhaps not unexpectedly, then, Van Gogh's shoes (albeit by means of a 'detour' which unsettles conventional ideas of direction) provide the leverage for Heidegger then to show how the truth of an entity comes in the work to stand in the light of its being; how the art work finds both dynamic unity and repose through the paradoxical mixture of conflict and design, rest and motion, 'setting up' and 'setting forth' that we find where truth in art is 'setting-itself-to-work' in the *Riss* of earth and world. Of course, by way of such a paradoxical interplay between movement and stasis, struggle and rest, Heidegger's conception of truth in art indeed founds itself on an idea of leverage; although as we have seen for Heidegger (as for Derrida) such leverage occurs only in the aporia of founding, only in the aporetic question of foundations or origins. Already (and for how long now?) we are setting off towards, setting up or stepping within the question of the institution.

Step three: Derrida's 'Restitutions'

In the context of his remarks on orientation in thinking within the university occuring towards the end of 'Mochlos', Derrida suggests that, 'as Kant will have told us, the university will have to go on two feet ... two feet *with shoes*, since it turns on an institution, on a society and culture, not just nature' (p. 31). (Derrida remarks elsewhere that 'you do not say a pair of feet. You say a pair of shoes',[6] as if everything to do with pairedness is instituted and needs to be analysed as such: we will come back to this.) Derrida's evocation of *shod* feet orients his essay in its final stages towards 'a discussion' held with Meyer Shapiro some years earlier 'on the subject of certain shoes in Van Gogh', a discussion concerned with 'the Heideggerian interpretation' of the painting (pp. 31–2). The debates indicated here between Derrida and Shapiro and Shapiro and Heidegger (already and once more we seem to be tracing out a series of steps) are set in motion in Derrida's 'Restitutions', the last part of *The Truth in Painting*. Here Derrida finds himself 'witnessing, not without taking part in it', a 'duel' between Heidegger and Shapiro (as the back cover blurb would have it). What sort of leverage exerts itself in the space of these two or three steps?

In a paper first published in 1968 entitled 'The still life as a personal object', Meyer Shapiro offers a reading of 'The origin of the work of art' which he dedicates to his colleague Kurt Goldstein, 'who first called my attention to this essay'.[7] Here Shapiro disputes Heidegger's attribution of Van Gogh's shoes to a peasant and by extension takes issue with the supposed authenticity of the rural landscape, the pathos rooted in the call of the earth and the labour of the field, and in fact the entire folk world which Heidegger presents as the truth of the painting. At the time of Heidegger's lectures forming the substance of 'The origin' (1935 and 1936) all this was, of course, 'not foreign to what drove Goldstein to undertake his long march to New York, via Amsterdam', as Derrida puts it (pp. 272–3). Against Heidegger, then, Shapiro insists that the shoes in the painting belong not to the peasant's feet rooted in the soil but to Van Gogh himself as – by this time – an uprooted city dweller, an exile. By wresting the shoes from the earthy world of the peasant portrayed so eloquently by Heidegger and restoring them as property to the dispossessed emigrant, Shapiro's paper does much more than pay homage to Goldstein as a valued colleague. Restituting the shoes to the signatory of the painting (retying the shoes to the signature), the essay dedicates itself to, as Derrida puts it, 'the immense tide of deportees searching for their names', victims of the violent upheavals of techno-industrial modernity culminating in mass warfare; and indeed to the 'army of ghosts demanding their shoes', those chillingly anonymous shoes piled up at Auschwitz (p. 329).

While he is keenly aware of the political stakes involved in Shapiro's critique of Heidegger, and the 'duty' or 'debt' it supposes, Derrida nevertheless detects in this dispute between the two not only an oppositional struggle but a certain 'correspondence', an exchange but also something like a common interest. For both, 'the desire for attribution is a desire for appropriation' (p. 260): that Heidegger assigns the shoes to a peasant and Shapiro to the city-dwelling artist is in either case 'properly due' neither to peasant nor painter but to these 'illustrious Western professors' themselves, so that the attribution in fact restitutes itself to them. This is not simply to suggest that Shapiro and Heidegger are somehow disingenuous or egotistical in falling upon these shoes only to establish their own academic credentials or repute. More than this it indicates that attribution and restitution occur only 'via a short detour' (p. 261), a period of carriage however brief, an investment and expense of energy however slight, which troubles the very idea of intact return, unstinting reparation, undisputed property. Yet upon such an idea of absolute restitution, it would appear, rests the truth in painting (of either the 'city' or the 'fields', the industrial or rural world) that both Heidegger and Shapiro wish to restitute. Indeed, the dispute concerning attribution does not happen solely due to Heidegger or Shapiro but occurs only by way of a certain leverage exerted between the two 'illustrious Western professors'. The 'restitution trial' (as Derrida calls it) walks on two feet, as it were, so that attribution/restitution is no more 'properly due' to either of them than to painter or peasant (pp. 260–1). (Indeed, amid these property disputes, neither would it be possible to restitute the picture solely *to itself* since, as Shapiro reminds us, Van Gogh painted a series of shoes, each a sort of step in a sequence, each acknowledging some debt to the others.)

To go further, it is clear that while Shapiro wishes to uproot Van Gogh's shoes, to dislodge the groundedness he feels Heidegger attributes to them, by way of an identification with the shifting and transient world of the modern metropolis, Shapiro's act of restitution in fact regrounds the link between representation and reference in that it assumes an unstinting identification between the subject and object of the canvas, sealed by painting's signatory: Van Gogh's shoes are the shoes of Van Gogh. This tautological situation of course means that, far from roaming the itinerant pathways of the exile or emigre, the shoes can go nowhere. They're not only grounded, they're rooted to the spot, stuck. Shapiro therefore restitutes the shoes in the form of leaving them where he finds them (that is, with Heidegger or the unchanging ground associated with the peasant world). He restores them to the eternally dispossessed through a procedure of repossession that means they can never properly be returned. Thus, the way in which Shapiro claims the shoes' proper ownership in fact destines them to remain disputed property.

Shapiro's procedure seems thoroughly disoriented in that he reproaches Heidegger both for being too referential (for Shapiro, Heidegger restitutes truth to the shoes by grounding them in an authentic peasant or folk world with all its dubious politico-ideological connotations) and for being insufficiently referential (neglecting to delimit the pictorial specificity of the shoes within a series of paintings by Van Gogh, according to Shapiro Heidegger fails to see that the actual picture he analyses was painted once Van Gogh had abandoned the 'fields' for the 'city': thus Heidegger's attribution is foiled by nothing but an absolute literalism which supports Shapiro's contention that Van Gogh couldn't have painted peasant shoes in Paris). Notwithstanding this apparent contradiction, Derrida shows how Heidegger's own procedure for establishing or 'presenting' truth in 'The origin' is in any case not as referential as his critic often supposes, and certainly less so than Shapiro's rather incongruous recourse to a sort of crude empiricism or literalism as a way of uprooting the shoes. Reading the essay more carefully, Derrida notes that the example chosen to illustrate Heidegger's intention in 'The origin' is not at bottom a specific picture but more generally a 'product', or, in Hofstadter and Kuhns' translation, 'a common sort of equipment' (p. 663). As 'product' or 'equipment' Van Gogh's shoes are in fact only an 'accessory' within a much wider project of asking how truth manifests itself. As I suggested earlier this entails a question of nature or origins that, in the very process of its asking in Heidegger's essay, resists or disputes decidability, attribution, firm grounding, reference. This is because the equipment (intermediate between 'thing' and 'work') that is needed to keep the question open compels us to remain perpetually in transit, always stepping within the circle. For Derrida, then, Heidegger's larger aim in attributing the shoes to peasantry 'via' a painting by Van Gogh is not really to reground and fix the link between reference and representation by taking (a) painting as an illustration; or even, for that matter, is it principally his aim to establish or ground reference solely by way of the emergence of 'peasant' truth. Once the shoes are taken as product or equipment instead of 'picture', Derrida contends:

> The 'same truth' could be 'presented' by any shoe painting, or even by any experience of shoes and even of any 'product' in general ... It is not the truth of a *relationship* (of adequation or attribution) between such-and-such a product and such-and-such an owner, user, holder, bearer/wearer-borne. The belonging of the product 'shoes' does not relate to a given *subjectum*, or even to a given world. What is said of belonging to the world and the earth is valid for the town and for the fields. Not indifferently, but equally ... art as 'putting to work of truth' is neither an 'imitation', nor a 'description' copying the real, nor a 'reproduction', whether it represents a singular thing or a general essence. (p. 312)

Heidegger's shoes belong in no particular place – 'belonging to the world and the earth' calls to mind the *Riss*, the rift at the heart of belonging or design – and with no particular person, be they a specific individual or a representative figure. Paradoxically enough, this precisely is the nature or essence (the truth) of their belonging within the Heideggerian scheme. Rather than existing as a picture that illustrates truth deeply rooted elsewhere, enabling repatriation to a native land by means of an indisputably correct signpost (the very notion of reference), as 'product' or 'equipment' the shoes cause truth to appear only as a condition or function of the never-ending transit that characterises both the painting of shoes travelling from one exhibition to another and Heidegger's own procedure of stepping within the circle. While Heidegger's shoes belong to no particular place or person, then, Shapiro's case on the contrary 'calls on real shoes: the picture is supposed to imitate them, represent them, reproduce them. Their belonging has then to be determined as a belonging to a real or supposedly real subject' (p. 312). From Derrida's point of view (if that were possible in a text written as 'polylogue') a profound disorientation therefore occurs as a condition of the leverage exerted within the dispute between these two 'illustrious Western professors': Heidegger's shoes, far from grounding themselves in the peasant world, 'belong' with the 'uprooted emigrant', the dispossessed outcast; while Shapiro's shoes, far from being restituted to the exiled and anonymous victims of modernity, are placed firmly on the side of 'the rooted and the sedentary' (p. 260).

The proofs submitted therefore prove nothing ('*nothing proves they are peasant shoes* ... nothing proves or can prove that "they are the shoes of the artist, by that time a man of the town and city"' (p. 364)) so that once more restitution founders on its own intention, as it were. Retying the shoes to the picture's signatory by way of a tautological knot (Van Gogh's shoes are the shoes of Van Gogh), Shapiro presents the artist 'face on' or face-to-face with his own footwear (p. 348). The shoes face Van Gogh facing the shoes: Shapiro ties the tautological knot tighter, by means of the attribution of the shoes to a subject and subjecthood to the shoes, as if to ensure beyond any reasonable doubt their fit or fittedness. Yet, as everybody knows, it is impossible (if like Shapiro you insist on proper usage) to put on a pair of shoes while they are facing you. It is precisely at the moment of absolute identity, indisputable attribution, pure restitution, perfect fittedness – *because of it*, if you like – that the shoes cannot be claimed, put on, made to fit. Shapiro fittingly demonstrates that shoes tied too tightly can trip you up. The play of putting on/putting off, attachment/detachment, usefulness/uselessness therefore becomes an important theme for Derrida, one I will return to presently.

There might be (or, as Derrida says, 'there will have been' (p. 257)) a correspondence between Heidegger and Shapiro, but this may not be quite enough to fashion them into a pair. While Derrida finds 'something like a pairing together in the difference of opinion' (p. 263) that sparks the quarrel in the first place (Heidegger turns out to be doing what Shapiro supposedly wants to do; Shapiro turns out to be more like the Heidegger with whom he takes issue than Heidegger himself), nevertheless 'a pair functions/walks (*marche*) with symmetrical, harmonious, complementary, dialectical oppositions, with a regulated play of identities and differences' (p. 377). As we have seen, the disagreement between Shapiro and Heidegger neither takes the form of dialectical struggle nor a regulated play of difference and identity but instead walks with two left (or two right) feet. This is because the positions adopted or ascribed on either side of the dispute take on a similar appearance to one another owing to the fact that both function in a self-contradictory or non-self-identical way. To schematise this a little in terms of the idea of walking, the left foot (Shapiro, say) asserts itself only by acting like the right foot (Heidegger) which, in turn, turns out to be more left than right. This gives the impression of a bizarre sort of perambulation. However, since neither foot is simply left nor right (or, which amounts to the same thing, the feet are at the same time both left and right) we can say that the dispute itself has two left (or two right) feet.

This state of affairs in fact corresponds with a problem in Van Gogh's painting that is nowhere visible in the dispute itself. As Derrida shows, both the professors (rushing along like Jameson) assume too hastily that the shoes in the painting form a pair. This much does not constitute a point of disagreement between them: indeed, it has to be agreed upon for the dispute to take place. At a certain level, for Derrida, Heidegger and Shapiro need to assume that the shoes in question form a pair so that they can go about the business of attribution, fitting the shoes to the feet of one subject rather than another, or indeed using them more generally as equipment to carry out a certain kind of restitution. But what makes them so sure the shoes are a pair? 'The more I look at them,' says Derrida of Van Gogh's shoes, 'the less they look like a ... pair' (p. 278). It is difficult not to agree with him. Shapiro and Heidegger therefore *institute* the shoes as a pair (and for Derrida, we might recall, a pair is always instituted). Yet on the basis of this assumption of a pair of shoes the professors return or restitute to them not undisputed truth but the dispute itself; a dispute 'walking on two [left or right] feet' which, in truth, corresponds with (and therefore returns itself to) the undecidability of the shoes as a pair. More widely, this would imply that an institution cannot be restituted to itself in its institution, that the institution founders on its own founding.

However, the unpairing or dis-pairing that causes the institution to lose its footing among its own foundations is not simply a cause for despair. While two right shoes or two left shoes cannot be put on or used 'without injuring the wearer, unless he has the feet of a monster' (p. 374), we have already seen in Heidegger the radical monstrosity, hybridity, impurity of shoes as equipment (intermediate between 'work' and 'thing') demanding a properly improper usage if a step within the circle is to be taken. Thus the unpaired shoes occupy and expose a kind of supplementary space or margin in the discourse on – indeed in the nature of – shoes, which in fact turns out to be fundamental and originary. The institution (in the form of a pair) is based, founded, on a monstrosity (two left or two right feet) which nevertheless need not – indeed cannot – simply be negatively marked if one acknowledges that orientation in its conventional sense and positive value in any case seems inescapably disoriented, inhabited by its other, therefore being just as monstrous or hybrid. The unpaired shoes, like Frankenstein's monster, are cut out and sewn back together, and like the *Riss* of earth and world they cut out (rift) but also sow back together (design) the pair, since the pair is not just absolutely different from them but also in a certain way the same. (Both the professors' pairs are monstrous in this Frankensteinian way: Heidegger severs a single painting from a series in order to attribute, restitute or institute the pair, says Shapiro; while Shapiro himself cuts out of Heidegger's long essay twenty or so lines, 'snatching them brutally' (p. 285) says Derrida, to attribute, restitute, institute the pair otherwise.) The unpaired shoes therefore do nothing as simple as destroy the institution. More complexly, they also seem to repair it, sow it back together, in the monstrous form to which it in any case properly (improperly) belongs.[8]

To come back to the play of putting on/putting off, attach-
ment/detachment, usefulness/uselessness in Derrida's essay, then:
this is understood not in terms of oppositional conflict or absolute
confrontation, but on the basis of a non-self-identical doubleness
characterising each pair (undecidably two left or two right feet).
Here we find not simply 'the logic of a cut', not a straightforward
detachment which leads to a 'logic or even a dialectic of opposition'
but, in the play of attachment/detachment, a double bind or
'the interlacing of *differance*', of laces tied neither too tightly nor
loosened to the extent that they unbind (p. 340). In Heidegger's
'The origin', for example, the truth of the useful (the product or
equipment) appears 'in the instance of the out-of-service' (the idle
and, as we have seen, uselessly unpaired shoes painted by Van
Gogh). That truth appears in this way in fact overloads uselessness
with value, although of course this '"truth" of the truth is not useful' just as 'the "truth" of the product is not a product' (p. 346). The
uselessness of the institution (both the institution of the shoes as a
pair that cannot be restituted to its institution, and the institution of
oppositional pairing that likewise cannot be restituted to itself) thus
turns out to be useful, or at least usefully useless/uselessly useful. To
borrow and adapt Robert Young's terms, this useful uselessness/
useless usefulness might 'function as a surplus' that the economy of
the institution, both inside and outside the university, may not comprehend.[9] Yet, far from simply ruining the institution, this useful
uselessness/useless usefulness in some way repairs it, not by restoring an original state of health but by returning the institution to (the
paradox of) its originary monstrosity. For, like Frankenstein's creature, the university always institutes itself as a figure of dis-re-pair.

The blinking of an eye

I want to conclude by pursuing a connection between disoriented
footing in the university and the question of vision. This connection
between vision and footing is of course implicit in the essays we have
covered so far, all of which look at the painting of shoes.
In Jameson, shoes are regarded and (almost, although not quite)
discarded in a postmodern wink of an eye, so that the Jamesonian
gaze rehearses uncritically the unstable and problematic relations

of attachment/detachment, putting on and putting off, we find under consideration in Derrida's 'Restitutions'. Heidegger suggests that shoes in Van Gogh, rather than providing a pictorial illustration upon which the critic might fall in order to reveal truth, in fact show truth or cause it to appear. Van Gogh's shoes are not just inspiring objects to be looked at. As equipmental beings they themselves body forth a vision of truth. This shift of emphasis reverses the subject-object relation so that when speaking of the shoes as formed matter, as product or equipment, Heidegger remarks, 'Usefulness is the basic feature from which this entity regards us' (p. 659). Retying the shoes to the picture's signatory by way of a tautological knot (Van Gogh's shoes are the shoes of Van Gogh), Shapiro presents the artist 'face on' or face-to-face with his own footwear. The shoes return the artist's look since Shapiro's tautological knot entails attributing the shoes to a subject by means of assigning subjecthood to the shoes. In a sense, then, it is not just that Van Gogh has a vision of shoes. Rather, by being possessed of eyes the shoes restitute the artist's vision to himself. This recognition, then, marks a certain correspondence with Heidegger. For Derrida, however, the shoes do not simply produce or restore vision. They also bring about 'this blindness, this putting-to-sleep ... of all critical vigilance' (p. 279), at the moment Heidegger and Shapiro simply assume and agree on the pair. Indeed, as Shapiro and Heidegger 'bet on the pair' in the form of a dispute where each can be found always outbidding the other, the correspondence, as we have seen, '*tightens itself* to the point of self-strangulation' (p. 376). Of course this would be the point at which the eyes pop out, speculation putting an end to itself in the specular. This interplay between vision and blindness appears elsewhere in Derrida's work. For example, in 'The principle of reason: the university in the eyes of its pupils' (a paper which in its very title sets up a speculative, specular play between vision and the institution, sight and knowledge), Derrida speaks of:

> Opening the eyes to know, closing them – or at least listening – in order to know how to learn and learn how to know: here we have a first sketch of a rational animal. If the University is an institution for science and teaching, does it have to go beyond memory and sight? In what rhythm? To hear better and learn better, must it close its eyes or narrow its outlook? In cadence? What cadence? Shutting off sight

in order to learn is of course only a figurative manner of speaking. No one will take it literally, and I am not proposing to cultivate an art of blinking. And I am resolutely in favour of a new university Enlightenment (*Aufklarung*). Still, I shall run the risk of extending my figuration a little farther, in Aristotle's company. In his *De anima* (421b) he distinguishes between man and those animals that have hard, dry eyes [*ton sklerophtalmon*], the animals lacking eyelids, the sort of sheath or tegumental membrane [*phragma*] which serves to protect the eye and permits it, at regular intervals, to close itself off in the darkness of inward thought or sleep. What is terrifying about an animal with hard eyes and a dry glance is that it always sees. Man can lower the sheath, adjust the diaphragm, narrow his sight, the better to listen, remember, and learn. What might the University's diaphragm be?[10]

As with his essay 'Mochlos', Derrida notes in this paper that the founding of the university cannot be treated as a self-begetting 'university event', in the same way that the founding of the law is not simply a judicial question, one either of 'legality' or 'illegality'. Therefore the institution built on the principle of reason is also built 'on what remains hidden in that principle', so that the 'principle of reason installs its empire only to the extent that the abyssal question of being that is hiding within it remains hidden, and with it the question of the grounding of the ground itself' (p. 10). Just as footing is found on uncertain foundations, so the vision of the university proceeds from what remains concealed. However, this raises the question of responsibility in that critics, professors, academics working at 'multiple sites [on] a stratified terrain' with 'postulations that are undergoing continual displacement' need to observe 'a sort of strategic rhythm' playing itself out between the 'barrier' and the 'abyss', between the protected horizon, the secured partition, of the university space and the invisible and unthought bottomless chasm on which this is founded (p. 17). The 'strategic rhythm' that pulsates between the barrier (horizon of vision) and the abyss (hidden and unseen) provides a way to play one off against the other: such 'playing off' as the responsibility of the critic or academic appears partially to redeem speculation. Derrida associates this 'strategic rhythm' with 'the blinking of an eye'. The same 'strategic rhythm' or 'blinking of an eye' is called for in the antagonistic interplay between end-oriented and fundamental research. If the university can only found itself on what remains hidden and abyssal, then end-oriented, useful research always proceeds on the basis not only of a repression but also an exploitation of foundations that in fact must remain fundamentally invisible, unthought, useless. However, if goal-oriented or useful research is therefore structurally reliant (i.e. founded) on the preservation of what is abyssal, unfathomable, unyielding, then useless or 'basic' research can no more be simply opposed to its end-oriented counterpart. As Derrida points out, fundamental research frequently becomes 'indirectly reappropriated, reinvested by programs of all sorts' (p. 16); and indeed by refusing to recognise goals often finds itself unwittingly 'serving unrecognized ends, reconstituting powers of caste, class or corporation' (p. 18). 'Beware of ends; but what would a university be without ends?' (p. 19) Derrida asks. The instituting of the university in terms of the 'barrier' or protected boundary, often conceived of as a precondition for non-interference by intrusive forces external to the university, itself necessitates the positing of limits and ends. Paradoxically, fundamental research may go beyond but nevertheless can only happen within the horizon of the university. Research itself, never simply either basic or goal-oriented, useless or useful, founded on the visible horizon or on an indomitable blindness, thus calls for the 'strategic rhythms' of 'the blinking of an eye' not dissimilar to 'walking on two [undecidably left or right] feet'.

The university's vision, neither hard-eyed and vigilant nor blindly asleep but produced by the rhythms of blinking, therefore institutes itself as a hybrid not unlike the always disrepaired monster. The shadow of Frankenstein's creature in fact casts itself over Derrida's essay:

> During more than eight centuries, 'university' has been the name given by a society to a sort of supplementary body that at one and the same time it wanted to project outside itself and to keep jealously to itself ... with the relative autonomy of a technical apparatus, indeed that of a machine and a prosthetic body, this artifact that is the university has *reflected society* only in giving it the chance for reflection, that is *dissociation*. (p. 19)

As a figure both of attraction and repulsion, of attachment and detachment, cutting out and sowing back together, the monstrous institution of the university renders possible a self-reflection which is also always a projection. The university therefore consitutes itself in the form of a risk (a risky invention). Playing off one against the other blindness and insight, reflection and dissociation, the members of this improper body (cut out and stitched back together) are perhaps best placed to witness the (dis)orienting play of difference and identity that arises from a look in the mirror:

> The time for reflection is also the chance for turning back on the very conditions of reflection, in all the senses of that word, as if with the help of an optical device one could finally see sight, could not only view the natural landscape, the city, the bridge and the abyss, but could view viewing. (p. 19)

Notes

1 Jacques Derrida, 'Mochlos', in *Logomachia: The Conflict of the Faculties*, ed. Richard Rand (Lincoln, NB and London: University of Nebraska Press, 1992), pp. 31–2.
2 Properly speaking, for Derrida a pair of shoes cannot be the object of a fetish. In 'Restitutions' (see note 4) he draws our attention to the fact that it is a lone shoe, no longer functioning according to 'the law of normal usage' (p. 333) as part of a pair, no more caught up in the reproductive (heterosexual) play of paired opposites, that comes to be associated with the monstrous 'perversity' of the fetish. However, following Derrida I argue in this chapter that the attribution of pairedness to Van Gogh's shoes cannot restitute the institution of the pair to itself, but instead unwittingly reveals the shoes as undecidably either two left or two right feet. In order to contest or prove the pair and thereby effectively repress the anxious sight of two left or two right feet, both professors in the 'restitution trial' witnessed by Derrida in *The Truth in Painting* want to attribute the pair either to a feminine or a masuline identity: Heidegger attributes the pair to a peasant woman, Shapiro to the male artist. The debate itself institutes this heterosexually paired opposition. But to the extent that the institution of the pair cannot be restituted to itself, the fetish cannot wholly be disregarded or repressed in the dispute that takes place over Van Gogh's shoes.
3 Frederic Jameson, 'The cultural logic of late capitalism', in his *Postmodernism, Or, The Cultural Logic of Late Capitalism* (London and New York: Verso, 1995), p. 4. All further references will be given in the main body of the text.

4 See Jacques Derrida, 'Restitutions of the truth in pointing [*pointure*]', in his *The Truth in Painting* (Chicago, IL and London: University of Chicago Press, 1987), p. 263.

5 Martin Heidegger, 'The origin of the work of art', in *Philosophies of Art and Beauty: Selected Readings in Aesthetics from Plato to Heidegger*, ed. Albert Hofstadter and Richard Kuhns (Chicago, IL and London: University of Chicago Press, 1976). All further references to Heidegger's essay will be given in the main body of the text.

6 Jacques Derrida, 'Restitutions', p. 264. All further references will be given in the main body of the text.

7 Meyer Shapiro, 'The still life as a personal object', in *The Reach of the Mind: Essays in Memory of Kurt Goldstein*, ed. M. I. Simmel (New York: Springer Publishing Company, 1968).

8 The monstrous indeterminacy of shoes is also traced out by the double-edge which fashions them and by which, on a last, they are fashioned. Derrida remarks, 'like a glove turned inside out, the shoe sometimes has the convex "form" of the foot (penis) and sometimes the concave form enveloping the foot (vagina)' (p. 267). This monstrosity of undifferentiated difference, as it were, is confirmed by the anxiety the shoes cause Freudian thought. Derrida notes that Freud insists, 'certain symbols cannot be *at the same time* both masculine and feminine' but 'he does so only to admit immediately afterwards that bisexual symbolization remains an irrepressible, archaic tendency' (p. 268), i.e. somehow primal or originary. Undifferentiated difference as exemplified in the sexual monstrosity of the monster-shoes to some extent explains why, as I note above, in order to contest the pair and thereby repress the traumatic vision of two left or two right feet, both participants in the 'restitution trial' wish to attribute to the pair either a feminine or a masculine identity: Shapiro attributes the pair to the male artist, Heidegger to a peasant woman. The debate itself institutes this heterosexually paired opposition. Furthermore the pairing of shoes in this way sheds light on why a lone shoe, no more caught up in the reproductive (heterosexual) play of paired opposites that establishes 'the law of normal usage' (p. 333), comes to be associated with the monstrous 'perversity' of the fetish.

9 Robert Young, 'The idea of a chrestomathic university', in *Logomachia*, ed. Richard Rand, pp. 121–2. Young's arguments arise in the context of a discussion of the antagonistic interdependency of the 'useless' and the 'useful' traditions of the English university. 'Useless' learning refers here to longstanding Oxbridge traditions of disinterested study, and the rather unworldly pursuit of truth and beauty founded on classical literature as a means to cultivate gentlemanly character rather than develop professional skills. 'Useful' university education indicates an apparently different and opposed tradition emerging properly in the nineteenth century; a tradition

associated with the names of Smith and Bentham, and devoted primarily to technical and vocational training. Nevertheless, as literature becomes institutionalised as an object of academic study around the turn of the century, the learning associated with traditions of 'uselessness' seems most useful in combating what Arnold envisaged as anarchy on the horizon of urban, industrial, materialist society. Equally 'usefulness', end-oriented study or sheer vocationalism in its most extreme form, might be thought to accentuate specialisation and concomitant effects of social alienation, thus hastening capitalism's eventual decline – the worst sort of 'uselessness'.

10 Jacques Derrida, 'The principle of reason: the university in the eyes of its pupils', *Diacritics,* 13:3 (1983) 3–20, p. 5. All further references will be given in the main body of the text.

CHAPTER 2

The 'glasse' of majesty: reflections on new historicism and cultural materialism

While in the 'restitution trial' of Van Gogh's shoes a correspondence can be found between the two 'illustrious Western professors' Heidegger and Shapiro, each in some sense suggesting that the footwear in question actually produces or restores vision, we have seen that Derrida detects in the dispute between them a certain 'blindness', a 'putting to sleep ... of all critical vigilance'. The bidding and outbidding that occurs on the basis of an assumption of pairedness 'tightens itself to the point of self-strangulation', a point where the eyes rupture and burst. However, Derrida does not simply despair of the advent of vision within sleep or the muddling of insight with blindness. Instead, in 'The principle of reason' he affirms the more productive possibilities of, as it were, the unpaired pairing or non-self-identical doubleness of these apparent opposites, played out speculatively in the 'strategic rhythms' of 'the blinking of an eye'. This sort of vision, not unlike the idea of 'walking on two [undecidably left or right] feet', institutes itself as a kind of Heideggerian equipment, an intermediary, a hybrid. By means of 'the blinking of an eye' the co-extensivity of reflection and dissociation that institutes (the vision of) the university can be witnessed. In this way, Derrida suggests that the university could be imagined as an 'optical device' with which we 'could view viewing'. Such self-reflexive viewing would not render visible a clear, transparent vision of the kind customarily associated with enlightenment. Instead, through 'the blinking of an eye' the optical device of the university would equip us to speculate on the unstable, continually shifting interplay of blindness and insight, sleep and vision, instituted within or upon it. It would equip us to observe (to witness, to respect) the disorienting play of reflection and dissociation, identity and difference, that happens when we take a look in the mirror.

In this chapter I want to affirm the importance of this kind of vision, by tracing some of the counterproductive, self-defeating effects that occur when such a disorienting interplay of identity and difference, reflection and dissociation remains more or less unwitnessed (or disavowed, projected elsewhere) by critics. Unwitnessed, apparently displaced, it nevertheless remains, casting a ghostly shadow over academic effort and work. Here, while disorientation is literally dis-regarded rather than viewed or utilised productively in the way Derrida suggests, nevertheless it stays to haunt those seeking 'new' or 'radical' forms of orientation ostensibly founded on a repudiation of other directions. The 'new' or 'radical' kinds of criticism I want to discuss in this chapter have by different means pointed the way for various assaults on 'ahistorical', 'apolitical' deconstruction over the last few years. Yet the 'founding' texts of new historicism and cultural materialism in fact furnish useful examples of, as it were, disregarded disorientation, in that they deny other directions, robustly orient themselves, exert leverage, in what amounts to a hall of mirrors.

The boundaries of criticism have been redrawn in the last twenty years or so by new forms of historicism and politically charged critique which, despite their differing motivations and methodologies, share a fundamental similarity in that they deny the transparency of the 'object' of study and thereby repudiate a longstanding view of the intellectual as dispassionate, discriminating and aloof in any reading of literary or cultural forms. Thus, both new historicism and cultural materialism, in recognising the part played by criticism itself in the representation of its subject matter, have produced analyses which can be seen to blur the borderline between the 'seeing self' of the critic and the 'image' of the thing studied. However, there are several problems with this ostensibly radical opening-up and crossing of the frontiers between the critic and the object. For one thing, it has often been noted that, despite various complex theorisations of the inseparable relationship between the object and activity of criticism, new historicism has largely been characterised by an apoliticism in which can be located traditional kinds of scholarly detachment. Similarly, while on one front cultural materialism rejects the 'otherness' of history in order to use the past as a platform for arguments of topical relevance and contemporary political intervention, on another its critique of more conservative readings of literary texts frequently requires, strategically, a forceful insistence on the clear difference between the radical critic and the reactionary target under attack. Far from simply pushing back conventional boundaries, then, these forms of criticism can often be found to operate according to a restless oscillation between sameness and difference in relation to their objects.

As this chapter will argue, such a restless oscillation between the sameness and difference of subject and object, the 'seeing self' and the seen image, can often be traced within a 'hall of mirrors' image of power, usually located in the early modern past, that emerges from new historicist and cultural materialist readings. Moreover, in ways not fully understood or accounted for within these approaches, the textual and historical forms on which new historicism and cultural materialism have concentrated provide, in themselves, a mirror in which to view the problems associated with these forms of criticism, throwing up spectral images which indeed haunt contemporary perspectives. In particular, the shifting and unstable relations of identity and otherness structuring the relations between the king (or power) and the subject in the early modern period – the 'object' of a great deal of attention in recent years – can be seen, in the mirror imagery of Renaissance rulership, to constitute problems of authority and legitimacy that also affect and indeed entrap historicist and political criticism today.

The spectacle of power

In a number of key texts associated with new historicism and cultural materialism, the 'hall of mirrors' image of the spectacle of power is considered so important as to provide a starting point for the analysis. The introductory chapter of Jonathan Goldberg's *James I and the Politics of Literature* (1983), for example, depicts the monarch as an actor-spectator in court masque, positioned and represented doubly as the focal point and focusing eye of the spectacle in progress. Indeed, the notion of majesty as both a representational mirror and a perspectival gaze is one which recurs throughout Stephen Orgel's ground-breaking book *The Illusion of Power* (1975), where he writes, for instance, 'The king must not merely see the play, he must be seen to see it'[1] and furthermore, 'Masques are the expression of the monarch's will, the mirror of his mind'.[2]

This mirror imagery similarly characterises Stephen Greenblatt's account of Holbein's *The Ambassadors* that begins *Renaissance Self-Fashioning* (1980), a reading that seems greatly influenced by Foucault's interpretation of Velasquez's *Las Meninas*, with which *The Order of Things* (1966) opens. In both of these accounts of Renaissance portraiture, moreover, there appears as a condition of their very existence as mirror systems a blind spot at the centre of powerful structures of identification and reflection: Velasquez's invisible canvas of origination, and Holbein's oblique, unseeable image of finality or death. The double representation which emerges from this mirror imagery – of the subject-object relation as both circular or reversible and somehow discoupled from a final point of origin, a foundation or a cause – is not, however, limited solely to new historicism. It relates also, for instance, to Jonathan Dollimore's important cultural materialist book, *Radical Tragedy* (1984), which argues that the subject in non-essentialist terms is always already inscribed within systems of power (although in a sense of course this replaces one kind of essentialism or ground with another), but also that power decentres identity, producing discontinuity within its own, nevertheless limitless, frame of reference. Moreover, the myriad reflections which unfold and circulate within the 'frame', whether constituted as a political or aesthetic space, are found in all these texts, through the continual decentring of the centre, to spill over, ensnare and implicate the spectator and by extension the reader or the critic within the field of Renaissance representation: the mirror image paradoxically constituting what it reflects. From this perspective, the relations of identity and difference, doubleness and discontinuity that currently enter into or structure descriptions of the 'object' must surely also be explored in terms of the effect they have on the workings of the criticism which describes them. Before attempting this exploration, however, it is worth looking more closely at the spectacle and imagery of Renaissance power with which new historicism and cultural materialism have remained fascinated, to examine the political functions and implications of its structure of representation. This is not to return to the idea of history as an external, stable or authentic ground, acting straightforwardly as a single point of origin or departure in linear terms, since in the particular instance I want briefly to look at – James I's accession, and the literature written to celebrate it – power circulates primarily through an image of the spectacle of kingship as an almost groundless play of representation, an interminable scene of mirroring and symbolic doubling. However, since I want to retain the possibility – for reasons that will become clearer later on – that this 'hall of mirrors' image of power is not simply the product or characteristic of recent critical formulations, that it might have a different sort of agency in which the problems of contemporary criticism may be located, it seems worth going 'outside' the pages of new historicism's and cultural materialism's key texts (although of course, in its doubleness, the scene of early modern power is not, as we will see, just an 'outside') in order paradoxically to reflect on them, to find their blind spot.

In Thomas Dekker's entertainment given to James I in 1604, the massed subjects gathered to behold the acceding monarch's entrance to London are termed 'the glasse alone, Where the neate Sunne eache morne himself attires'.[3] The royal 'Sunne' as an eye narcissistically perceives its object as a reflection of 'self'. James as a sun is placed at the origins of the subject's vision, his solar energies enabling the spectatorial gaze into being, pre-empting – ideologically or discursively, at least – effects of dissocation and fragmentation at the scene of rule, since every look is represented as conditional on the prior presence of the sun-king. At the same time, however, majesty is portrayed foremost 'in' its object, deriving power precisely as an image in a mirror. This circular play of origin and representation between the ruler and the ruled constitutes a powerful and authorising metaphysics. Writing of the masque particularly in 'Love's triumph through Callipolis', Ben Jonson remarks that 'All representations, especially of this nature in court, public spectacles, either have been or ought to be the mirrors of man's life'.[4] Thomas

Middleton, in his entertainment to the new king, speaks expansively of James as the 'Mirror of our times'.[5] The twinning of monarch and 'man' (or 'our times') through example and imitation enables an inclusive and totalising image of power to be forcefully reinscribed.

The circularly double representation of origins produced within the solar-specular imagery of Jacobean rule represses – but also implies – the absence of a representation of power's origination. The eternally lost beginnings of power suggested by Hobbes's post-Revolutionary political philosophy here enables a mystification of the presence of kingship, therefore achieving what seems an invaluable ideological function. However, since the identity of ruler and ruled resists dissociation within this structure of representation, the masses are – in the very image of the king – invested with mysterious, unrevealed power. Thus Samuel Daniel's 'Panegyric congratulatory' in honour of James's accession is preoccupied with 'clouds' and 'shadows' that threaten to 'obscure the light' of the regal sun. Tellingly, it is those subjects nearest to power, closest to the royal star, who are imagined to harbour dark designs in this poem, wishing to 'embroil the State' in slander and confusion.[6] In another panegyre, the king is urged by Jonson on his first entrance to Parliament to cast his 'searching beames ... to pry' into 'darke and deepe concealed vaults' permeating the nation's substratum, where 'men commit black incest with their faults'.[7] Here, the solar imagery of power is utilised to expose difference, deviation and deceit, rather than to identify sameness and unity. This shift produces a confused representation of the subject-object relations of power, in which majesty – itself implicated through metaphysical doubling and mirroring in the infrastructural depth and universality of dark origin and purpose – struggles to break free from its own self-image; to represent the 'other' which exists nonetheless at the origins of its own identity. If the mirror constitutes its reflection, then it is in the context of these problems of projection, displacement, disavowal and return that I want to read new historicist and cultural materialist readings of the Renaissance.

New historicism

For some, new historicism can be situated within an American tradition, epitomised at its height by New Criticism, that seems primarily concerned with the 'cultivation of "emotional distance"'.[8] Thus, for example, Graham Holderness in a recent article in the *Times Higher Education Supplement* remarks that new historicists appear less interested in political intervention than detached academic interpretation.[9] However, others do not associate with new historicism this sense of detachment. In the Bloomsbury *Guide to Renaissance Literature* (1992) edited by Marion Wynne-Davies, the entry for new historicism declares, 'It is essential to understand that new historicists do not assume that literature reflects reality and that these "reflections" enable the reader to recover without distortion that past represented in the texts ... we read texts from the perspective of our own age'.[10]

This sense of being implicated in the reading of literature or history suggests an unremoved stance that certainly seems to be present in the introductory chapter of Stephen Greenblatt's *Shakespearean Negotiations* (1988). This attempts, unusually, to provide some insight into the operations – rather than just the goals – of new historicist methodology. Greenblatt tells us at the outset, 'I began with the desire to speak with the dead'.[11] This desire projects the critic toward a horizon at which the sense of separation is almost entirely overcome. The idea of the past as a lingering ghostly trace serves mythically to entwine and even to coalesce the subject and object of criticism, fantasising an eerily direct, metaphysically oral exchange between the whispering eternal spirit of literature and the peculiarly clairvoyant voice of the critic: a voice in effect encountering its own echo.

Such a self-reflexive conjuncture, however, tends to struggle free from all context, mediation or 'outside' interference. Greenblatt to some extent recognises that his desire to couple together subject and object obstructs an articulation of the specific strategies both of historically constituted texts and critcism itself: that it actually *hinders* the sense of implication that might be expected from it. Yet his chapter remains conspicuously full of doubles. Shakespeare's plays are brought to life, Greenblatt senses initially, because of 'a sublime confontation between a total artist and a totalising society' (p. 2); between the complete artistic genius and the almost Tillyardian social totality in which all parts exist via inclusion and organic exchange only in relation to the whole. Nevertheless, Greenblatt discards these parallel, monolithic concepts in favour of a deconstructive image of the writer as 'constructed out of conflicting and ill-sorted motives' (p. 3) and a loosely Machiavellian or Marxist view that 'Elizabethan and Jacobean images of unity seemed like anxious rhetorical attempts to conceal cracks, conflict and disarray' (p. 2). This reconsideration serves, however, only to replace one double with another: the now fragmented and decentred Shakespeare none the less *wholly* reflects the representation of Renaissance culture and society as plural and contradictory. Indeed, this perverse similitude gives fresh license to what Walter Cohen has called new historicism's methodological principle of 'arbitrary connectedness', which conceptualises difference within 'generalising influences'.[12] Its avowed abandonment of the foundational principles of structure or the supposed grander narratives of theory effectively enables new historicism to argue the legitimacy of linking cultural fragments to one another in almost any pattern. From this perspective, as has often been noted, a tenacious formalism unfettered by any traditional historical sense seems paradoxically to return, enabling an inclusive model (one of limitless linkages) to be sneaked in by the back door of new historicist criticism, working against the grain of its anecdotal descriptions of the marginal, the erratic, the partial and the fragmented. Here, as in the scene of Jacobean accession that we looked at before, the representation of difference is confounded within the very same discursive formation that seeks to emphasise it.

However superficial it may be on closer inspection, 'the cost of this shift of attention' toward fragmented structures is, Greenblatt tells us, 'the satisfying illusion of a "whole reading"' (p. 4). The processes of doubling we have traced so far here reach a further stage of completion, as the representation of criticism itself comes to mirror the image of its literary and cultural objects. It is paradoxically by means of the absence of a 'whole reading' governed by received models of thought that an inclusive model can be salvaged and the bits put back together as reflections of one another, a unifying line drawn between the fragments. Greenblatt's rather fashionable emphasis on discontinuity, contradiction and the active processes of exchange of 'social energy' in culture and across history is therefore undermined by a series of conceptual twinnings which threaten to render the relations of author, culture and critic inertly mimetic. In speaking with 'the voice of the other', Greenblatt states in conclusion, 'I had to hear my own voice' (p. 20). This can be read in two ways. At one level, Greenblatt at last seems willing to be audible in his own readings of literature, culture and history, enabling the trace of mediation to appear in any representation of the object. However, this encounter can be seen ultimately to work the other way round. The doubleness invoked by the metaphysical echoing of voices that initially provides the impetus for writing (Greenblatt's 'desire to speak with the dead') can be seen, despite the critic's attempt to distance himself from it through the stress on fragmentation, to constitute the structure and methodology of Greenblatt's chapter. In this context, hearing one's 'own voice' in the 'voice of the other' suggests an overwhelming lack of separation, a groundless reverberation, in which the representation of critical practice becomes once more inconspicuous and unobtrusive in the representation of Renaissance forms, just as it had been in traditional positions of scholarly detachment.

It has been suggested that this unself-consciousness has caused new historicists to recreate within their own discourse the forms of power they seek to criticise. As Jean Howard has put it – in a metaphor that resonates suggestively with the very dilemma of Renaissance rule – new historicism, by representing its objects in its own image, has paradoxically displayed an inability 'to reflect upon itself'.[13] Alan Liu has observed that 'the New Historicist "Renaissance" is coincident with the corridors and vaults of the postmodern intellect'; that its imagery rather blindly reflects the concerns of the contemporary American professional mind 'in its academic confines' seeking, as Louis Montrose writes of seventeenth-century individuals and groups, 'possibilities for limited and localised agency within the regimes of power and knowledge'.[14] Montrose's configuration of the limitations inherent in the subject–structure relation in the Renaissance thus corresponds powerfully with those in which the critic is felt to exist in the present, so that this view of the early modern past can be seen to reinscribe such limitations as much as it seems to seek out 'possibilities'. From a similar viewpoint, it can be seen in Greenblatt's work that concepts of transaction, circulation and exchange, when mooted in conjunction with notions of dynamic 'social energy', come to reflect a cultural poetics of the market that prevailed in 1980s America.[15] Indeed, the inability to break out of this kind of language within a form of analysis that presents itself, however tentatively, as progressive or politically 'different' relates once again to the inescapable mirror imagery of power identified – by new historicism itself – in the early modern past. Indeed, while new historicism was still in its heyday during the latter part of the 1980s, it was remarked by Don E. Wayne that, unless Greenblatt *et al.* reconsidered their methods, intentions and assumptions, they risked limiting themselves to a 'fascination with the same imposing spectacle' – the spectacle of the 1980s – mirrored projectively in history.[16] But this recognition did not allow for the possibility that new historicism may not have got trapped simply in the hall of mirrors of the present, but also of the past: a past or a 'beyond' encountered not just in oppositional terms as an 'outside', but one that operates in supplementary ways 'in-between' (that is, both 'doing' and 'undoing' the relation between) formations of subject and object, identity and otherness.

Presumably to open up and confront the contextual influences on his work, Greenblatt remarks in 'Towards a poetics of culture' (1989) that 'the oscillation between totalisation and difference, uniformity and ... diversity ... unitary truth and a proliferation of distinct entities' – an oscillation he finds in the different views of late capitalism held by Lyotard and Jameson – depends 'less upon poststructuralist theory' than upon the 'poetics' of contemporary American culture and politics.[17] The impetus here seems to be to short-circuit the notion that the agency of culture can somehow be reduced to postmodern games of language or formations of theory (although, tellingly, it is only through a reading of the 'theory' of Lyotard and Jameson that this refutation is made). Nevertheless, Greenblatt's own methodology – which in this essay is discussed implicitly in terms of establishing preconditions for the description or representation of culture which it paradoxically names as external to 'theory' – operates precisely within and by means of the very same 'restless oscillations' between difference and sameness, as we have seen in the opening chapter of *Shakespearean Negotiations*. Such unstable shifts between 'distinct entities' or 'discontinuous discourses' on the one hand, and 'totalisation' or 'monologic unification' on the other – while located here within a circumscribing, contextual present – are not only indicative of Greenblatt's own confused manoeuvrings, but double up in his work to provide a means of representing the problem of Renaissance power, particularly through the notions of circulation, social energy and containment. Thus, even before an analysis of the object is undertaken, these terms come to describe a 'restless oscillation' in new historicist thought and representation between the doubles of history and modernity, culture and criticism; that is, between distance and proximity, otherness and presence, between what is 'outside' and what is interior to one's discourse: an oscillation which suggests an affinity with the very problem of authority and authorisation we find in the early modern display of power. It seems to me that recognising this affinity does not simply repeat Greenblatt's sleight of hand in projecting a constitutive 'inside' (his own methodological fluctuations) as an 'outside' agent (cultural poetics/politics), since the scene of Renaissance rule is itself a structure of representation which, through its complex patterns of mirroring, renders uncertain and undecidable the boundaries between inside and outside to begin with. The instability of its doubling effects at the level of representation problematises, displaces, suspends the originary, external and authoritative status of the Renaissance spectacle of power as much as, within the terms of my discussion of the factors influencing the formation of contemporary theory, it might seem to be emphasised. However, it is precisely because of the shifting ground of the scene of Renaissance rule as an economy of representation blurring the distinction between inside/outside that an affinity between its patterns of formation and those of contemporary criticism can be rethought in terms of a Derridean notion of supplementarity rather than by way of any kind of causal logic or teleological narrative.

Such a relation between history and criticism can be found ranging in different ways across Greenblatt's rather imperious introductions to new historicist volumes. In his foreword to *The Power of Forms in the English Renaissance* (1982), Greenblatt writes, 'Renaissance literary works are no longer regarded as a fixed set of texts that are set apart from all other forms of expression and that contain their own determinate meanings or as a stable set of reflections of historical facts that lie beyond them'.[18] This repudiation of literary forms as independently objective entities, together with a confident denial of any determinable relation of texts to 'historical facts' in effect allows the identity of literature (or, by extension, historical culture) to take shape only in conjunction with – as a condition of – criticism. From such a vehement decentring of the text we might expect a critical self-consciousness of the kind often valorised by new historicists to emerge. But there remains an ambiguity and blindness in this ostensibly radical, double location of meaning, which can be traced by comparing, for example, the content of a volume like *Representing the English Renaissance* (1988), a collection of articles from the new historicist flagship *Representations*, with Greenblatt's introduction to it. In one essay, 'The sovereign, the theater, and the kingdome of darknesse: Hobbes and the spectacle of power' by Christopher Pye, the scene of Renaissance rule is described – in terms very similar to those with which we began – as an imaginary structure of solar reflection which represents the spectatorial gaze of the subject as inevitably a condition of the illuminating, sun-like presence of the ruler.[19] Within this solar imagery, the origins of the subject's thought and being are deeply immersed in the double and decentring trace of representation through which power self-reflexively circulates. By ruling out any reality that might 'lie beyond' its own unbounded frame of reference, the spectacle of power is therefore very much a scene of disempowerment also. As Greenblatt puts it in his prefatory remarks, this representational doubling is the means by which 'power is alienated and transferred irrevocably to the sovereign'.[20] But isn't this also the means by which authority is transferred from the essay to the editor's introduction? And, more important, doesn't the formation of Renaissance power described by Pye suggest an analogy with the double location of meaning found in new historicism's representation of the object?

Cultural materialism

Cultural materialism very much claims at the gritty level of practice as well as in the seductive language of theory to foreground its – and others' – mediations of literary and cultural objects. By way of various appropriations of Althusserian and Gramscian notions of ideology, it distinguishes cracks, gaps, differences and transformations in the relations of these objects to various forms of criticism and performance, while attempting not to present itself as a separate or detached entity. Indeed, cultural materialism has been situated within a British tradition of criticism characterised by 'a far greater orientation toward the present and toward political concerns';[21] changing the strident undertaking of Leavisite criticism for overt political commitment. Yet, within the context of this commitment, does cultural materialism make its interventions in a thoroughly self-aware analytical manner, fully exposing the shifts and repetitions that occur between criticism and its objects? Jean Howard has observed that Jonathan Dollimore's view of Elizabethan drama as offering 'a recognition of the discontinuous nature of human identity and its social construction' suggests an affinity between 'this picture of the Renaissance and certain contemporary understandings of our own historical moment as the post-humanist epoch in which essentialist notions of selfhood are no longer viable'.[22] Cultural materialism, she argues, finds in the early modern period 'a self-consciousness about the tenuous solidity of human identity' which encourages 'playfulness with signifying systems' that cannot be entirely fixed, marshalled or contained. Howard argues that this image of the past resonates powerfully with 'some of the dominant elements of postmodern culture'. From this point of view, cultural materialism re-enacts new historicism's tendency to 'see an image of the seeing self' in its objects and representations. Robert Young suggests that this structure of reflection is crucial to cultural materialism since it enables its proponents to argue the contemporary relevance of their historical findings:

> Where yesterday's historian looked for the history of an oppressed working class, today's historian looks for marginalised groups, and those who have transgressed social norms ... they can now be retrieved to offer a potential that has a contemporary, that is

twentieth-century, political relevance. To this extent we could say that the cultural materialists re-assert a form of reflection theory, where history has become a mirror in which contemporary political priorities have been substituted for the former certain ground of Marxist analysis.[23]

In *Radical Tragedy*, one of the key texts in the development of cultural materialism, Dollimore refutes textual coherence and stresses instead literary and cultural fragmentation and discontinuity in the Renaissance. Yet he also suggests a surprisingly direct relationship of the postmodern to the early modern 'mind'[24] and indeed assimilates poststructuralist theories of difference, which facilitate an emphasis on decentred identity, to representations of history that seem to remain in thrall of cultural materialism's commitment to the 'form of reflection theory' described by Young. This equivocal stress both on disjuncture and resemblance might be seen from a broadly deconstructive viewpoint to demonstrate the contradictory presence of otherness and identity, the discordant interplay of sameness and difference, that constitutes Dollimore's own 'text'. However, there seems to be no space to confront or explain this methodological discordance in a book which, in its descriptions of power as both ever-present and discontinuous, otherwise rejoices in it at the level of the object of analysis. Instead, rather like the doubled, shifting and always displaced source of the sun-king's power, it remains hidden, a blind spot, in a vision (a reflection?) based almost entirely upon it. It is in this sense that *Radical Tragedy* confirms Young's assertion that 'criticism, like literature, remains uneasily poised between subversive and repressive functions'.[25] This contradictory positioning means that 'no critical position can be intrinsically political' or unambiguously aligned. The identity of cultural materialism as 'radical' would appear, from this perspective, to be entirely dependent upon its enactment of forceful repressions.

This problem of the politics of political criticism is crucial to any critical repesentation of cultural materialism. If cultural materialists generally do strive harder than their new historicist counterparts to represent fully the traces of difference between subject and object, criticism and text, in their readings of literary and cultural forms, these traces seem to fade or blur in their representation of the political. Cultural materialism rejects constructions of an inside/outside model in its view of politics, to represent itself in the image of the political. Politics is not treated as an object upon which criticism seeks to act from a traditional academic subject-position of distance and dissociation. Instead, it is represented as itself a kind of subject or agent, a means of constitution, representation and transformation similar to criticism itself. The supposed possessive power of politics/criticism as a subject or agent is partly the reason why cultural materialism can imagine itself to *be* 'political'; why, ostensibly, there can be a 'politics *of*' cultural materialism.

However, the doubling of politics and criticism can produce unwanted effects. In her contribution to the collection of essays *Political Shakespeare* (1985) – 'the most important book in the formation of cultural materialism'[26] – Margot Heinemann discusses the former Chancellor Nigel Lawson's conservative view of Shakespeare, espoused in an interview given to the *Guardian* in September 1983. Lawson claims that Shakespeare, possessing deep understanding of human nature, advocates order and degree as primary social virtues. Presumably Heinemann, as a cultural materialist, is committed to the political value and use of literature: the foreword to this volume speaks of cultural materialism's 'unwillingness to pretend to political neutrality'.[27] Yet Heinemann cannot fully disguise what is her moral indignation at Lawson's appropriation of literature for political ends. What would appear to be an uneasy doubling of the political critic and the politician is, however, earlier explained away by the editors. 'Cultural materialism does not, like much established literary criticism, attempt to mystify its perspective as the natural, obvious or right interpretation of an allegedly given textual fact', they insist. The difference between Lawson and the political critic would thus seem to be clear: cultural materialism does not seek to naturalise or objectify its political stance. Yet Heinemann refutes Lawson's outlook by arguing that he quotes his examples 'wholly out of dramatic context'[28] which she then goes on assiduously to recover. This manoeuvre in fact seeks, as Robert Young has put it, to 'reground the link between representation and reference that has been questioned by the semiotics of the last twenty years'.[29] Heinemann effectively claims that her reading is more 'true' to its object than her adversary's, and thus mystifies her perspective as 'the right interpretation of an allegedly given textual fact'.

Here, cultural materialism seeks to disidentify with the political, struggling to break free from politics in the sense of (false) ideology which it now stands against. To enact its political criticism, cultural materialism must expose reactionary positions on literature and culture by showing them to be politically motivated rather than 'natural, obvious or right'. But to distinguish itself from these reactionary positions, it feels compelled to repeat the mystificatory stance of reference, truth and legality (note the legalistic tone of 'allegedly') which it criticises in others, and against which, in principle at least, it defines itself. Thus, that which would ground or legitimise political criticism simultaneously shifts its foundations elsewhere, locating them in an image of 'otherness' it seeks to expose and undermine. A startlingly similar effect occurs in Walter Cohen's essay, 'Political criticism of Shakespeare' (1987). Cohen observes that the political in his essay refers to reactionary 'government power' and oppressive politics of 'race, class and gender', but also 'polemically designates only critical or oppositional work'.[30] This constitutive duality of meaning of the political is also apparent in *Radical Tragedy*, where Dollimore states that 'a current political engagement with Shakespeare is inseparable from what others have already made Shakespeare mean ... what those others have done with it is as political as what [radical criticism] is doing'.[31] While Dollimore's recognition of the embattled origins of (all) criticism is persuasive, for Cohen this defining of radical critique in terms of its 'other' gives rise to theoretical and political anxiety.

Cohen attempts to disentangle the awkward twinning of institutional power and radical protest in his concept of the political by suggesting that, whereas reactionary positions are characterised by a false, mythological claim to truth, oppositional politics reveals and possesses an actual truth in demythologising truth claims. This argument is unself-consciously paradoxical, however, and fails to differentiate the identity of the political. It traps Cohen in a position where he is forced to claim that the leftist 'partisanship' of recent 'political writing on Shakespeare' is 'not only compatible with but also necessary to a commitment to objectivity and scholarship';[32] yet this realigns radical criticism with oppressive ideology, which seeks to represent its 'partisanship', its politics, as true. Cohen's retreat into 'objectivity and scholarship' constitutes the contradiction of political criticism's recoil from its Hydean double of false politics. It signals a return to the apolitical, judicial image of the intellectual that underpins traditional forms of criticism attemptedly rejected by cultural materialism – rejected, ironically, for cloaking politics in claims to authenticity and truth.

These examples therefore reveal a tendency in cultural materialism to inscribe and indeed authorise itself according to a double and contradictory position. Cultural materialists might contend that primarily they do not seek but rather scorn authority, and that these individual acts of criticism should be viewed more sympathetically (and perhaps less 'theoretically') in terms of a struggle against authority rather than for it. However, it seems undeniable that cultural materialism's identity *as* 'radical' is itself legitimised only within, and perhaps because of, the kinds of inconsistent impulses we have looked at. In order to differentiate itself from politics in the sense of oppressive ideology, to define this politics as 'other', it experiences the desire to break free from the political – the necessarily slanted, partial and yet self-justifying representation of a supposed reality – which constitutes simultaneously its self-image and that of its hated alter-ego. It is indeed within the very process of (or attempt at) differentiation that an uncanny identity between the patterns of formation and self-presentation of the two emerges.

Finding itself implicated in its double in ways it had not anticipated, cultural materialism's effort to free itself from its own self-image, to represent the 'other' which exists nonetheless at the origins of its identity, brings us back once more, ironically in the grip of a process of repetition, to the metaphysical relations and problems of Renaissance power with which we began. The image in a 'glasse' serves doubly as source and privation of identity, suggesting blindness as well as insight, ataxia as well as enablement. This ambiguity is inextricable, since – as we saw in Jonson's own terms – the double is darkly incestuous, committing 'black incest' with its own 'faults'. From this point of view it is possible to entertain a departure from the usual critique which declares that new historicism and cultural materialism say more about their own problems and concerns than they do about their supposed objects of study (literature, culture, history) or fields of intervention (politics). Rather, within a somewhat different view of the subject–object relation here, it may be more productive to suggest that these forms of criticism have remained trapped within the same representation – and crisis – of authority with which, perhaps not coincidentally, they have remained fascinated.

The power of spectacle

The 'glasse' of majesty depended on the reversibility of subject-object within the drama of Stuart succession, in order to reproduce and circulate the mythic totality of power. This also depended on the undifferentiation of the image and the object, the indistinguishability of reflection and source, so as to ensure the *absence* of myths of origin – which otherwise only provoked questions of legitimacy – during celebratory scenes of unbroken continuity and full immediacy that found no space for them. Within this fluid interplay of mirror and self, entity and sign, the theatre of rule confounded scrutiny since, by denying all forms of decathecting the object within a timeless moment of pure presence, it not only precluded the possibility of independent positions, but more fundamentally ruled out interpretative discourse altogether. By restoring the spontaneously self-referential identity of image and referent, signifier and signified, the spectacle of Jacobean power redeemed the lack on which language is predicated, and aspired almost to its redundancy as a form of recording experience. Speaking of the entrance made by James and his entourage to London, Michael Drayton remarked that:

> None ther's could judge a witness of this sight
> Whether of the two did take the more delight
> They that in triumph rode, or they that stand
> To view the pompe and glorie of the land
> Each unto each other such reflection sent[33]

This bewilderment of language occurs since the mirroring of king and subject closes the critical distance from which interpretative discourse would be possible. Thus Drayton's verse repudiates itself as commentary and instead rejoices blandly in its own confusions. By the same token, Middleton's depiction of the king as 'Mirror of our times' paradoxically elevates James 'Above the world and all our human wits'. The poet concludes by asking 'what pen, Or art, or brain, can reach thy virtue then?'.[34] The king as an uninterrupted expanse of proximity, presence and plenitude – a veritable mirror of the times – here becomes unrepresentable within the subject's language, while at the same time existing enigmatically at the very origins of the subject's being. In this sense, alienation becomes the strange effect of wholeness and reconciliation. But it is an alienation which for this reason, unfree in speech and finding only emptiness in words, cannot speak its name. And which instead, through its perplexed sense of identity and tremulous voicing of platitude, teeters precariously between repetition and impending silence, unable to acknowledge the complex antinomies characterising its position. Here, perhaps at last, we find reflections of the present in the 'glasse' of majesty.

Notes

1 Stephen Orgel, *The Illusion of Power: Political Theater in the English Renaissance* (California: University of California Press, 1975), p. 16.

2 *Ibid.*, p. 45.

3 Thomas Dekker, 'The magnificent entertainments', in *The Dramatic Works of Thomas Dekker*, Volume II, ed. Fredson Bowers (Cambridge: Cambridge University Press, 1955), p. 256.

4 Ben Jonson, 'Love's triumph through Callipolis' (l.1–3), in *Ben Jonson*, Volume VII, ed. C. H. Herford and Percy and Evelyn Simpson (Oxford: Clarendon Press, 1952), p. 735.

5 Thomas Middleton, 'Part of the entertainment to King James', in *The Works of Thomas Middleton*, Volume III, ed. A. H. Bullen (New York: AMS Press, 1964), p. 225.

6 Samuel Daniel, 'Panegyric congratulatory', in *The Progresses, Processions and Magnificent Festivities of King James I*, Volume I, ed. John Nichols (New York: Burt Franklin, 1966), p. 386.

7 Ben Jonson, 'Panegyre on the happie entrance of James our soveraigne to his first high session of Parliament', in *The Progresses, Processions and Magnificent Festivities of King James I*, ed. John Nichols, p. 421.

8 Walter Cohen, 'Political criticism of Shakespeare', in *Shakespeare Reproduced: The Text in History and Ideology*, ed. Jean Howard and Marion O'Connor (London: Methuen, 1987), p. 21.

9 Graham Holderness, 'Trans-atlantic views on changing world', *Times Higher Education Supplement*, 1075 (11 June 1993) 20–21.

10 Marion Wynne-Davies (ed.) *Guide to Renaissance English Literature* (London: Bloomsbury, 1993), p. 208.

11 Stephen Greenblatt, *Shakespearean Negotiations: The Circulation of Social Energy in Renaissance England* (California: University of California Press, 1987), p. 1. All further references will be given in the main body of the text.

12 Walter Cohen, 'Political criticism of Shakespeare', p. 27.

13 Jean Howard, 'The new historicism in renaissance studies', in *New Historicism and Renaissance Drama*, ed. Richard Dutton and Richard Wilson (London: Longman, 1992), p. 31.

14 Alan Liu, 'The power of formalism: the new historicism', *English Literary History*, 56 (1989) 733.

15 Richard Wilson, 'Historicising new historicism', in *New Historicism and Renaissance Drama*, ed. Richard Dutton and Richard Wilson, p. 9.

16 Don E. Wayne, 'Power, politics and the Shakespearean text', in *Shakespeare Reproduced*, ed. Jean Howard and Marion O'Connor, p. 60.

17 Stephen Greenblatt, 'Towards a poetics of culture', in *The New Historicism*, ed. H. Aram Veeser (London: Routledge, 1989) pp. 1–13. See p. 8.

18 Stephen Greenblatt, Introduction, in *The Power of Forms in the English Renaissance*, ed. Stephen Greenblatt (Oklahoma: Pilgrim, 1982), p. 6.

19 Christopher Pye, 'The sovereign, the theater, and the kingdome of darknesse: Hobbes and the spectacle of power', in *Representing the English Renaissance*, ed. Stephen Greenblatt (California: University of California Press, 1988), pp. 279–302.

20 Stephen Greenblatt, Introduction, in *Representing the English Renaissance*, ed. Stephen Greenblatt, p. xii.

21 Walter Cohen, 'Political criticism of Shakespeare', p. 21.

22 Jean Howard, 'The new historicism in renaissance studies', p. 21.

23 Robert Young, *White Mythologies: Writing History and the West* (London: Routledge, 1990), p. 89.

24 Jonathan Dollimore, *Radical Tragedy: Religion, Ideology and Power in the Drama of Shakespeare and his Contemporaries* (Brighton: Harvester Press, 1985), p. 3.

25 Robert Young, 'The politics of "the politics of literary theory"', *Oxford Literary Review*, 10 (1988) 131–57, p. 134.

26 Marion Wynne-Davies (ed.) *Guide to Renaissance English Literature*, p. 113.

27 Jonathan Dollimore and Alan Sinfield, Foreword, in *Political Shakespeare: New Essays in Cultural Materialism*, ed. Jonathan Dollimore and Alan Sinfield (Manchester: Manchester University Press, 1985), p. viii.

28 Margot Heinemann, 'How Brecht Read Shakespeare', in *Political Shakespeare*, ed. Jonathan Dollimore and Alan Sinfield, p. 203.

29 Robert Young, 'The politics of "the politics of literary theory"', p. 132.

30 Walter Cohen, 'Political criticism of Shakespeare', p. 20.

31 Jonathan Dollimore, Introduction to the Second Edition, in *Radical Tragedy*, pp. xiii–xiv.

32 Walter Cohen, 'Political criticism of Shakespeare', p. 20.
33 Michael Drayton, 'A paean triumphall', in *The Progresses, Processions and Magnificent Festivities of King James I*, ed. John Nichols, p. 425.
34 Thomas Middleton, 'Part of the entertainment to King James', in *The Works of Thomas Middleton*, ed. A. H. Bullen, p. 225.

PART 2

Institutions

CHAPTER 3

Excellence and division:
the deconstruction of institutional politics

Having raised the question of leverage in the context of a disoriented academic institution characterised by Derrida in terms of the motif of 'walking on two feet', and having examined also some of the effects that occur when critics try to disregard the disorientation that in various ways attends their academic work and effort, I want to turn now to two recent and important deconstructive studies of the university already mentioned in the introduction, in order to pursue the issues attendant upon a) the deconstructibility of an institutional politics of opposition, and b) the different challenges and possibilities afforded by the deconstructibility of the university's institutional set-up itself.

Excellence and 'thinking without identity': Readings

At a very early stage in his book *The University in Ruins*, Bill Readings recognises that the discourse of excellence which typifies, organises and represents the Western university in the late twentieth century is at bottom non-ideological, politically non-partisan, in orientation or determination. The 'dereferentialisation' of the modern institution with regard to an idea or content (reason or culture, for instance, as the keystones of the university after Enlightenment) means that, 'What gets taught or researched matters less than the fact that it be excellently taught and researched'.[1] This is not to imply that research and teaching are destined no longer to have 'political relatedness' with regard either to the university's inside or its outside, but merely that 'the nature of that relation is not ideogically determined'. In light of this realisation that contemporary academic effort and work takes place in an institutional environment undetermined from the outset as to 'political or cultural orientation', or even 'in relation to any instance of political power', Readings suggests a possible explanation for the kind of academic disorientation between left and right described in the last chapter:

> This is one of the reasons why the success of a left-wing criticism (with which I am personally in sympathy) is turning out to fit so well with institutional protocols, be it in the classroom or in the career profile. It is not that radical critics are 'sell-outs', or that their critiques are 'insufficiently radical' and hence recoverable by the institution. Rather, the problem is that the stakes of the University's functioning are no longer essentially ideological, because they are no longer tied to the self-reproduction of the nation-state. (pp. 13–14)

The end of the epoch of the nation-state brought about by the unstinting globalisation of late capitalism and the apparently irresistible rise of transnational corporations has, for Readings, been accompanied generally by a process of 'depoliticisation' characterised by 'the loss of belief in an alternative political truth that will authoritatively legitimate oppositional critique' (p. 47). This is because the modern or 'posthistorical' bureaucratic state is no longer fashioned on the basis of the traditional concepts and politics of national identity, but instead reproduces itself in terms of 'nonideological belonging' (p. 48). The 'managerial state' of the late twentieth century promotes a sort of social inclusion along the lines of 'a corporate identity' whereby participation occurs at the price of becoming an (efficient) operative. This tends to erode the established discourse and rhetoric of the subject or the citizen, recasting almost beyond recognition an historically specific ensemble of notions of contract and right. Readings suggests that the emergence of this non-ideological or, as it were, apolitically determined 'unipolar' state 'marks a terminal point for political thought'. As 'posthistorical' human societies develop, the institution of the nation-state no longer occupies the centre of our contemporary nexus or system of power relations but 'is now merely a virtual point that organises peripheral subjectivities within the global flow of capital' (p. 111).

In other words, with the decline of the epoch and grand narrative of the nation-state, the previously fundamental relationship between the state and the individual (understood variously in terms of long-standing conceptions of right, contract, etc.) is more or less dismantled, so that the question of political inclusion or exclusion with regard to the (political) centre becomes misleading if not obsolete. As Robert Young has noted, the dismantling of meaningful oppositional politics (in universities at least) during the Thatcher years in Britain depended in part on a disorientation that in a sense preceded it, whereby left-wing intellectuals and academics defended humanities departments and vocationally 'useless' degrees against swingeing government cuts by evoking a deeply conservative 'humanist belief' in the arts, cultural tradition, individual cultivation and so on.[2] Of course, at the theoretical level, many had questioned, resisted and tried to overturn this ensemble of ideas from the 1970s onwards, so that during the 1980s in British universities 'the oppositional literary and theoretical mode was not the oppositional institutional one'. Furthermore, for Young, the inconsistent stance of 'theorists' in this regard has meant that 'in attacking humanism, they have found themselves actually in consort with government policy'. Readings would underscore the point that this politics of opposition in the UK was not only doomed to failure owing to its intellectual incoherence and disorientation, but that it miscarried in practical terms because its mode and rhetoric of resistance at the institutional level relied heavily on an outdated view of the relationship of the individual to the nation-state (indeed of the identity of either), the obsolescence of which Thatcherism was both symptom and sign.

At best, then, attempts to articulate an alternative, oppositional, radical politics to the centre rest (disorientedly) on conservative nostalgia for a bygone era when narratives of redemption or liberation could be upheld in the face of tyrannical adversaries – now in fact superseded by an ideologically colourless 'unipolar', 'dereferentialised', 'managerial' state. At worst, such last-gasp radicalism (albeit artlessly optimistic) promotes a simulacrum of politics which – if conducted, taught, written or researched excellently enough – is likely to be endorsed and rewarded, rather than opposed, by the 'posthistorical' university, the 'managerial state', indeed capital itself. Dereferentialised in terms of a subject – of history, culture, or politics, for example – radicalism in the university cannot meaningfully ground or orient itself with regard either to the institutions of the state or even its own (desired) oppositional position. And yet, according to the principle of translatability combined with the 'generalised spirit of performativity' (Lyotard)[3] that characterises the mechanistically manufactured and technologically honed circuits of excellence, radicalism can be assimilated all too smoothly and efficiently as just another knowledge-commodity to be exchanged within the academic marketplace of the university. As Readings puts it:

> The University as an institution can deal with all kinds of knowledges, even oppositional ones, so as to make them circulate to the benefit of the system as a whole. This is something we know very well: radicalism sells well in the University marketplace. Hence the futility of the radicalism that calls for a University that will produce more radical kinds of knowledge, more radical students, more of anything. (p. 163)

The era of campus politics thus comes to an end with the decline of a situation in which the university is ideologically charged in relation to a nation-state or a politics of the centre. Once upon a time student protest could be pursued as a way to expose, resist, co-opt or disrupt the relays of political energy which, Readings suggests, flowed through the university as a reflection of a wider social mission. Now, as students begin to think of themselves primarily as customers or clients within the ideologically unaligned commercial university, the transmission of political ideals and the stirrings of political action are inhibited by an utterly transformed sense of belonging, having to do with ownership of learning on the basis of a contract (legal and economic but not political) with the institution.

In this context, Readings is sharply critical of attempts to salvage and renew traditional political radicalism in the face of the ruined institution of the modern university. Viewing as badly misconceived any effort to confront the machineries of excellence with the rhetoric of denunciation or nostalgia, he advocates instead a pragmatic rethinking of present and future possibilities for today's academics, in terms of developing survival tactics within the university, ways to 'turn the dereferentialization that is characteristic of the

posthistorical University to good advantage' (p. 122). With the onset
of the logic and discourse of excellence, notions of communicative
transparency within the more or less unified community of the
university advocated by the German Idealists – or indeed the
transactional models of communication within a horizon of consensus envisaged by the likes of Habermas – become more and more
untenable, even though the 'generalised spirit of performativity'
characterising excellence installs a (supposedly) cast-iron principle
of translatability. This paradox occurs because the traditional
concepts and paradigms of identity and unity that fashion the individual as expression of the institution and in turn the nation-state –
the very same paradigms that customarily organise and regulate the
relationship between individual disciplines and the institutional
formation of knowledge in general – are irredeemably eroded, as we
have seen in Readings' account, within the 'posthistorical' university. As the ideal of a communicative community wanes along with
the expressivist conception of the relationships between individual,
institution and state, discipline and university, Readings envisages
the possibilities of a 'community of dissensus'. This dissensual community, 'thinking without identity' (p. 127) and thus finding its very
conditions of possibility in the posthistorical university, would
nevertheless in practical terms remain unaccountable in regard to
the institutional logics and practices of accounting, audit, quality
control and so on that typify the bureaucratic and managerial exercise of excellence. While this dissensual community could only be
spawned by the posthistorical university, then, its temporality would
be entirely incompatible with the neatly packaged aims and objectives of excellence – its time management, its assessment methods,
its monitoring devices and performance indicators – precisely
because 'thinking without identity' would necessarily be 'systematically incapable of closure' (p. 128) and quite incomprehensible in
terms of the strictly calibrated measure of excellence. (Incidentally,
the non-sequentiality of the time it would take to think 'without
identity' the question of the university, beyond the measure of excellence, might itself be incompatible with Readings' historical narrative 'reason-culture-excellence' which, although it supposedly allows
for 'divergent and non-contemporaneous discourses' (p. 14), retains
a certain telos somewhat at odds with the dissensually non-linear

thought he advocates). 'Thinking without identity', without hope of termination, without the comforting anticipation of a final judgement, would (as I will argue in Chapter 6) entail maximal responsibility. Readings refers to this maximal responsibility in terms of '*keep*[*ing*] *the question of evaluation open*, a matter of dispute – what Lyotard would call the differend' (p. 130).[4] By keeping open the question of evaluation as a condition of 'thinking without identity', the dissensual community of the posthistorical university would – in view of the absolute and impossible responsibility taken upon itself – at every turn transvalue the evaluative procedures of excellence. It would do so from a 'standpoint' that could be located neither simply inside or outside the contemporary institution. Instead, the dissensual community 'thinking without identity' would necessarily mark and remark the incommensurability of the idealess posthistorical university with itself.

A similar argument could be made with regard to the interdisciplinary formation of the modern university (an issue that in various ways I attempt to stay with and think through in the last section of this book). In one respect, as Readings argues, the rapid rise of interdisciplinarity within contemporary academic institutions may have less to do than one might think with the development of new critical perspectives which take issue with traditional notions of the discipline, the canon, intellectual seriousness and authority, and so forth. Interdisciplinarity in its institutional formation frequently installs the very same principle of translatability that carries over the 'generalised spirit of performativity' noted by Lyotard into universalised evaluation criteria and techniques regulated only by the empty standard of excellence. In this light, Readings views with some suspicion the rise of cultural studies. Characterised by and large by a theoretical (or, one might say, politically progressive) commitment to challenging disciplinary hierarchies and institutional boundaries separating, for example, the academic from popular culture, cultural studies nevertheless facilitates an optimal number of interdisciplinary exchanges within the modern humanities, enabling excellence to regulate and assess academic work according to standardised evaluative criteria. (The idea that cultural studies in its 'dereferentialised' non-specificity is 'without a center of gravity' condemning it to a continual 'anxiety of orientation' (pp. 101–2) provides a context for my discussion in Chapter 5 of the insoluble disorientation between the activity and the object of criticism characterising cultural studies' institutional economy.) Nevertheless, this interdisciplinary formation of knowledge within the posthistorical university takes shape as a condition of the erosion of traditional paradigms of identity and unity that facilitate an idea of the discipline as an expression of the unified domain of knowledge or of the university. Thus interdisciplinarity, if it is 'without identity', not only panders to the contentless non-idea of excellence and its need for generalisable assessment criteria and administrative flexibility. 'Without identity', interdisciplinarity also potentialises – indeed one might say that it necessitates – certain kinds of academic work, thought, effort that exceed or subvert any calculable exchange between the particular and the general. In this case, interdisciplinarity remains, undecidably, both radically translatable and untranslatable with regard to the generalised discourse and practice of excellence. A certain alterity survives, holds itself in reserve, once more in the form of the modern university's incommensurability with itself. This 'useless' consequence of the (excellent) strategies of usefulness may provide one way of imagining a 'surplus', a remains, that the 'economy' of the university 'cannot comprehend' (Young, pp. 121–2). It is indeed interesting in this light that Readings advocates 'not a generalized interdisciplinary space but a certain rhythm of disciplinary attachment and detachment' which, while playing itself out 'without identity', never allows 'the question of disciplinarity', the question of the limits and effects of the systemic, to 'disappear' (p. 176). This rhythmic play of attachment and detachment calls to mind the very same unstable mix of the useful and the useless that Young discovers at the foundations of the modern university and, indeed, recalls also 'the interlacing of *differance*' that Derrida in 'Restitutions' attributes to the institution of the pair. This institution – rather like the modern university – can be taken as a figure of ruin but also fashions itself not unlike Frankenstein's creature as a figure of dis-re-pair, as we saw in Chapter 1, cut out and stitched back together in a way that affirms the monstrous hybridity, the non-self-identical doubleness, of the institution itself. Readings' 'rhythm of disciplinary attachment and detachment', not dissimilar to the rhythm of the blinking of an eye in Derrida's

'The principle of reason', thus installs itself at the limits of identity or in the very spaces of non-identity that at once enable and traumatise excellence.

This short account of Readings' book, while by no means exhaustive in terms of the many themes and issues it addresses, suggests that his analysis of the ruined university of excellence leads us back once again to Derrida's idea of (affirming) the academic institution as one that 'walks on two feet'. This is particularly the case in respect of Readings' insistence that the politics of opposition are inappropriate and inadequate to the situation in which the university finds itself. His attempt to imagine a dissensual community 'thinking without identity' amid the rhythms of 'disciplinary attachment and detachment' constitutes a bold effort to reaffirm the possibilities of leverage in the context of a disorientation of 'left' and 'right' within the non-ideological university.

Division and the deconstructible walls of the university: Kamuf

Peggy Kamuf's *The Division of Literature, Or, The University in Deconstruction* approaches the question of the university by way of a close analysis of the complex history of literary study in the modern university, reflecting on the problem of (the) institution by locating literary studies as a 'division' of the university – that is, as part of an institution that in important ways it partitions or describes. Here the institution of literature, set up 'through a decision within writing in general', sets aside a reserve to the extent that in 'each instituting decision' we find 'carried over the very mark of division as a kind of surplus that belongs to neither side of the division it marks';[5] a surplus-mark, then, that survives the deathly terminus of division (again, we will return to this in Chapter 6). In this sense it is conceivable that a division can be, at one and the same time, not a division since the instituted division, itself a kind of surplus belonging to neither side, cannot in fact exclude what it is supposed to exclude. In an enormously rich and diverse series of readings shifting between European and North American settings, dealing with (among other things) the educational reformers of revolutionary France, the writings of Gustav Lanson and Charles Peguy, Herman Melville's *The Confidence-Man* (1857) and the canon wars and PC debates of the 1980s and 1990s in the US, Kamuf pursues this issue of the 'division of literature' in terms of the impossible conditions of possibility of the institution's founding. While it is beyond the scope of this chapter to summarise exhaustively the wide-ranging historical and theoretical narratives underpinning Kamuf's study of the institution, I want – in the interests of some sort of dialogue with the work of Readings and indeed Young – to focus on the implications and effects, for Kamuf, of this unmanageable surplus or reserve of divisionality in terms of the deconstructible walls of the university itself.

In a chapter devoted to 'three moments in the formation of literary study as a separate domain within educational institutions' (p. 75), prefaced by a short reading of Locke's *Some Thoughts Concerning Education* (1693), Kamuf examines Hegel's speech of 29 September 1809 delivered to inaugurate Nuremberg's classical *Gymnasium*, and also the literary and art history of Taine and Lanson in France during the latter part of the nineteenth and the early twentieth century. These 'moments' for Kamuf can be seen to 'punctuate' in some way the history of literary study's institutional formation, 'between the emergence with the German romantics of the concept of literature and the overhauling modernization of the Western university under the aegis of science and principally historical science' (p. 75). Mindful perhaps of the a-sequential time it would take to think (in) the university beyond the measure of excellence, Kamuf is quick to remark that she is not concerned to 'reconstruct' this history in terms of a chronological or linear trajectory, but rather to underscore 'certain conceptual negotiations with the distinctions that would define this new institution'.

In Locke's essay, written prior to the institutionalisation of literary study within the field of academic knowledge, Kamuf finds a rejection both of the teaching of classical languages and of metaphysics and speculative philosophy on the grounds that they display a dire lack of useful, practical application. Locke singles out poetry in particular as hopelessly unworldly and quite profitless. Parnassus, he writes, has 'a pleasant Air but a barren Soil'. Here, of course, Locke asserts the futility of poetry by way of a somewhat trite poetic device, so that poetry becomes rather useful as a means to denounce poetic invention as vain and fruitless. Kamuf suggests that this is 'precisely the sort of divided gesture that turns up repeatedly in the vicinity of literature's or poetry's formation as a useful object of study' (p. 76). The repressed poetic returns in the very attempt to exclude poetry as a legitimate object of study in the tuition of gentleman, writing over exclusion 'as a species of inclusion' (p. 77), so that, precisely, the mark of division is carried over as a surplus that does not belong to either side of the division it marks. For Kamuf, this ambivalent play of inclusion/exclusion is equally pronounced in the academic, disciplinary institution of literary study. In fact, as Robert Young has shown with regard to British institutions in particular, the somewhat unstable interplay of the useful and the useless that crops up in literature's vicinity can be taken as exemplary in the fraught development of the modern university itself.[6] Kamuf is therefore quick to hint at the explanatory force of Locke's paradoxical repudiation of the literary or the poetic, in respect of the larger issue of the uneven, volatile, antagonistic interdependency that characterises the relationship between the arts and humanities and the scientific and technological faculties of the modern university. Thus the disciplinary institution of literary study, for Kamuf, might be seen to provide a convenient way to cordon off poetry's capricious and licentious energies and thus 'efface, forget, or suppress' (p. 77) the extent to which science and technology harness poetic invention to establish inventions of their own. Equally, the discipline of literary studies has colluded with its institutionally unstable position of, as it were, inclusive exclusivity insofar as it has attempted to borrow models from history and science in order to comprehend its special or distinctive object(s) of study.

A similar argument concerning the deconstructible walls of the university is made in relation to Hegel's rather implausible attempt in 1809 to persuade the worldly burghers of Nuremberg to support the newly reopened *Gymnasium*, founded on the classical study of Greek and Latin language and literature, in light of the recent closure of the *Trivialschule*, a popular modern institution devoted to the practical disciplines. Hegel advocates the setting apart of a classical literary education from technical instruction on the basis that, as the latter gains ground and threatens to hold sway, the former must be preserved as a matter of urgency in pure and uncontaminated form. As division is imagined to be in the service of purity, the school walls of the *Gymnasium* are set up by Hegel 'as a kind of protective barrier to keep out foreigners' (p. 79), as Kamuf puts it. However, Hegel then goes on in his speech to ally classical education to a process of cultural formation or *Bildung* that entails 'an encounter with the foreign and undigested'. The fiercely protected boundaries of the *Gymnasium* demarcate a protected zone in and from which, paradoxically, the active pursuit of *Bildung* necessitates the scaling of walls and the experience of foreign worlds in the interests of realising 'the true universal essence of spirit' (p. 80).[7] It seems that a kind of strategic censorship, always surmountable and yet continually required, provides the conditions for enlightenment's triumph over hitherto unknown and resistant objects (we will return to this presently). Kamuf thus writes: 'The dividing wall of *Bildung*, therefore, is itself divided between that which effectively separates or holds apart so as to prevent contamination, and that which poses itself as a separation only in order to be overcome' (p. 80).

The circuitous movement of Spirit among foreign worlds, culminating in a return to itself, leaves no wall standing in its wake. Spirit's movement surmounts the barriers and limits of translatability by subsuming alien or natural languages to the the universality of the concept. The dividing wall of *Bildung* sets aside foreign worlds only as the exteriorisation of Spirit's drive to realise its true universal essence, and thereby to return to itself. In this sense, as Kamuf notes, 'Spirit is never more at home than when it ventures into foreign lands' (p. 81). While giving a speech to mark the same occasion a year later, Hegel justifies the inclusion of military training exercises in the school curriculum – the result of a government decision imposed by force that would seem to impinge upon the protected zone of the academy and indeed upon the wholly nontechnical regime of a classical education – on the grounds that technical aptitude of the kind instilled by military training fosters a certain presence of mind that at times is more useful with regard to cultural formation than the speculative or reflective capacities of the mind. Here it is difficult to tell whether, in the movement of Spirit, 'mind' is being called by an internal impulse to assimilate that which exists outside it, or whether in fact the walls of the *Gymnasium* are being scaled *from* the outside, by order of government. As this

ambivalence works at the now fraying edges of the instituted division, once more we find a surplus carried over that belongs to
neither side of the dividing mark, a pollutant or admixture that nevertheless cannot be done away with since it facilitates the very
process of division. This surplus, then, at once underwrites and
overwrites the division between the literary and the technical,
between purity and foreignness, inside and outside, censorship and
enlightenment. Division thus redivides in the form or process of an
inseparable separation/non-separation; redivides, that is, in the form
or process of a (non-)division. The walls of the university are therefore deconstructible '*of and by* necessity' (p. 82), insists Kamuf. It is
not just that the hitherto sturdy archictecture of the institution
comes apart in the malign and tenacious hands of a skilled deconstructionist critic. Rather, the instituted divisions on which the university is founded founder in their very construction, not just to ruin
the university but to put it perpetually in a situation of (dis)repair
(as the example of Hegel's attempted accommodation of military
training within the *Gymnasium* curriculum clearly shows).

Kamuf notes that, while they doubtless contribute in their falter-
ing way to the fraught process of development of the modern
university, Hegel's walls (the walls of the *Gymnasium*) 'do not yet
delimit what we understand by a separate domain of literary study
in the university' (p. 84). Literature acquires disciplinary status
when it is comprehended as a distinctive object of knowledge as well
as an instrument of education. This requires, as Kamuf puts it, 'the
general sponsorship' of positivism that so characterises the modern
scientific university. She explores the effects of this positivism on the
institutionalisation of literature as a discipline by way of a kind
of case study of the work of Hippolyte Taine and Gustave Lanson
during the nineteenth and early twentieth century in France. Thus
Taine justifies the inclusion of literary studies within the university
on the strength of an analogy between the natural sciences and the
study of art, cemented by a classical idea of imitation whereby art
augments nature insofar as it reveals nature's (hidden) nature. Here,
within the instituted division of literature as a university discipline,
the analogical standing of art with regard to science itself divides
into two versions: i) the work of art is taken as an object of scientific study; and ii) art, like science itself, is not the product but the

process of production of objects for study. However, not only does
this second version of the analogy (in which the object of knowledge
is produced by the activity of study) simultaneously threaten the
supposed scientificity of literary study but, since the analogy functions as a surplus carried over on both sides of the division, it calls
into question, quite fundamentally, the objectivity of science itself.
Once more the deconstructible walls that spring up in literature's
vicinity not only cause an internal crisis for the disciplinary study of
literary texts but, of necessity, they expose the unstable foundations
of the modern scientific university itself. Similarly, Kamuf finds an
impure distinction between impressionism and method in Lanson's
attempt, during the early days of literature's disciplinarity in France,
to draw the boundaries of scientific literary historicism by endeav-
ouring on the one hand to banish altogether subjective impression
from objective methodology, and on the other recognising the need
to highlight (i.e. to retain or include) an inevitable degree of impres-
sionistic influence in order to limit and control it in the interests of
greater scientificity. In a passage that resonates strongly with
Derrida's description of the university 'walking on two feet', and
indeed which powerfully recalls the idea of leverage, Kamuf therefore suggests 'the institution of literary study is not a one-step but at
least a two-step process ... because the excluded term in the first step
is the included term in the second step' (p. 95). (This process is perhaps most clearly marked when Lanson contradictorily affirms the
distinctiveness of literary study in terms of the very same 'personal
elements' that he elsewhere disparages.) Hence, the instability that
characterises the institution of division(s) within the field of academic knowledge or the university 'cannot be worked out once and for
all but must induce repetitions with a certain regularity' (p. 95).

I want to stay with this notion of the regularly induced repetitions
that characterise the two-step rhythm or movement of institutionality, while returning to the broad question of freedom and limitation,
censorship and enlightenment, that has already cropped up briefly
with regard to Hegel. Kamuf, in another chapter, examines Kant's
distinction in 'What is Enlightenment?' (1784) between the private
and the public use of reason. Kant ties private usage to the exercise
of reason undertaken in one's capacity as a postholder or official
(for instance, a clergyman or military officer). Here, reasoned

argument and expression must sometimes be restricted in the interests of church or state, for example. In the public use of reason, however, such faculties can and must be exercised by the educated citizen – now thought of as distinct from any particular office held – without any such restriction. Yet Kant is conspicuously quiet on the subject of the responsibilities of private reason imposed by the civil institution and offices of the university. It would seem that the university presents a special case since the duties and obligations of the professional scholar correspond precisely to the exercise of reason that Kant elsewhere ties to public usage. In other words, as Kamuf puts it, 'private reason is indistinguishable from public reason' (p. 135) in the case of the institution of the university. Thus, the university would be the name for a division instituted within society that nevertheless marked a non-distinction or non-division between itself and publicness or indeed the public, the 'outside world', society.

Over a decade later, in *The Conflict of the Faculties* (1798), the university scholar nevertheless becomes subject to the very same distinction between the private and the public use of reason that earlier on Kant discards with respect to the university in particular. Having been refused permission to publish *Religion Within the Limits of Reason Alone* (1788) due to Prussian state censorship, Kant tries to reformulate the freedoms associated with the scholar's exercise of reason. Thus in *The Conflict of the Faculties* he reasserts, over and against his own recent experience of censorship, the unencumbered, unlimited expression of reason as a right of the university scholar. But it seems he can now do so only by means of drawing a distinction between, on the one hand, the strictures placed on public professors officially appointed to the institution of the university and, on the other, the freedom demanded none the less by Enlightenment thought. After 1788, Kant tries to retain and protect a space for the unfettered expression of reason, but this defence succeeds only at the cost of acknowledging the distinction between such public usage on the part of the university scholar, which should be unrestricted, and the private use of reason that necessarily obtains in a limited way with regard to his official capacity. Hence to preserve freedom and enlightenment, Kant has to reinstate the distinguishing mark or the dividing line that, paradoxically enough, limits reason's unrestricted exercise to public usage. The very condition of enlightenment's unimpeded progress is thus limitation or, in effect, censorship. Freedom of expression in the university is secured in *The Conflict of the Faculties* only at the price of a distinction between the public and the private use of reason that in fact underscores the idea of the university as a division officially instituted (by the state) within society, in a way that now seems to override the previous distinguishing mark of a non-division between the university and publicness (or society) itself. Thus, Kamuf tells us, 'the public discourse of the philosopher', whether it be supportive or critical of state policy, 'is not addressed to the public as such' but 'to their rulers' (p. 137): the direct and unmediated address to the public or the people that would seem at one point in Kant's writing to define the university over and against other official institutions is at another (here, in *The Conflict of the Faculties*) precisely to be mediated by the (divisive) state.

Here, then, the deconstructible walls of the university take the form of, in the first place, a division that does not divide (the university institution as distinctively the very expression of publicness) and, in the second place, a non-division that does (the unrestricted exercise of reason and carefully preserved scholarly pursuit of enlightenment requiring the distinction between private and public usage on which the university as an official, state-sanctioned institution rests). Again, we are in the midst of a two-step process that presumably 'cannot be worked out once and for all but must induce repetitions with a certain regularity'. Kamuf therefore chooses to 'recall Kant's analysis of public instruction in an age of enlightenment' (p. 138) in order to raise the question, today, of the university and the public. This she does in view of the PC wars and the debates over canonicity, multiculturalism, and literary theory in the university that have so occupied sections of the US media reflecting on questions of higher education during the last decade or so. In particular, Kamuf examines ways in which deconstruction is positioned at the very limits of coherence of this public discourse of the university: it is accused of being too political and not political at all by opponents on either side of the PC war, for example; and its practitioners are charged with holding to a doctrine that itself delegitimates fixed meanings, an allegation that allows journalists to feel justified in writing whatever they like, in a nevertheless doctrinaire way, about deconstruction! Such an incoherent positioning and representation of deconstruction signals, then, the deconstructibility of this so-called public debate. As with literature, the deconstructible walls or unstably drawn battle lines that spring up in deconstruction's vicinity reveal the divided and disoriented nature of all that stands against it: in this case, the public discourse of the university itself.

Deconstruction can be publicly censured only by the taking of certain liberties that in fact bind the offended party to the very same kinds of practices that they wish to condemn in deconstruction. Journalists and critics adopt an authoritative tone in saying whatever they like about deconstruction, yet in the process they fashion such condemnation in the very image of their idea of deconstruction as a manifesto for unlimited interpretation and sayability. Oppositionality is thus woefully disoriented, exclusion ironically overwritten as a species of inclusion. Craig Karpel, in his sweeping attack on deconstruction as a force for removing the limits of interpretation, for example, can be seen to 'censor the very permission he has been given' (p. 156) to write whatever he likes, attempting quite impossibly to summarise and dismiss contemporary French thought in the space of a very brief review. Recalling that in 'each instituting decision' (such as we are here associating with the publicly instituted discourse of the institution) one finds 'carried over the very mark of division as a kind of surplus that belongs to neither side of the division it marks', it can be seen that permission, license, freedom of speech within the public domain of a discourse on the university is inextricably tied to effects of censorship that cannot simply be displaced elsewhere and unequivocally opposed.

In the next chapter I want to explore in slightly different contexts this disorienting simultaneity and unstable division of enlightenment, license, freedom of expression on the one hand and limitation, restriction, prohibition, censorship on the other. Here, guided by Kamuf's emphasis on the deconstructible walls of the university, I shall examine debates about academic freedom and institutional censorship that have occurred during the 1990s around the issue of multiple submissions to scholarly journals, particularly in the United States. Here I will argue that the two-step processes associated with a university 'walking on two feet' do indeed 'induce repetitions with a certain regularity', and that these repetitions structure and regulate the interplay between enlightened, 'free' academic discourse and institutional censorship in a way that sustains the distinctively modern formation and legitimation of knowledge that begins to emerge in the early modern period. Hence in the second half of the next chapter I turn to Francis Bacon's *New Atlantis*, a text which itself envisages a somewhat disorienting passage to a New World and an apparently exemplary academy, to suggest that the non-oppositional formation of enlightenment-censorship highlighted by Kamuf sustains a rather fraught institutionality *in the very form of* the academy's unstable limits.

To recall once more the work of Bill Readings, my next chapter therefore suggests that the politics of opposition and the ideological 'exposure' of conservative forces are inadequate and inappropriate to the ruined or dis-re-paired circumstances in which the university finds itself. Yet by demanding that we think differently about the unstable and shifting, but nevertheless at times strategically functional, conditions of censorship and freedom in the academic institution, I want not merely to highlight the logical-conceptual inconsistency of the institution with itself but hint again at a surplus that survives the deathly terminus of division. It may well be the case that this surplus, reconceived as the hidden or the as yet unknown, is attemptedly carried over with a powerful frequency to sustain the continual process and progress of enlightenment. (I spend a great deal of time in the next chapter arguing as much.) Yet such a gesture of inclusion requires that this surplus be at the same time excluded, placed just beyond the threshold of the known in order that it be characterised as a 'new' object of enquiry – which in turn tends quickly to overwrite exclusion as inclusion within the field of knowledge. Once again the instituted mark of division redivides and exceeds itself in the form of an inadequately achieved distinction between inclusion and exclusion, separateness and non-separation, so that the ceaselessly shifting limits of the academic institution not only continue to prepare, repair and (re)orient it with regard to a (more or less predictable) future, but also open the university to the possibility of an *interminable* other, an unplaceable surplus-mark of division, beyond mere inclusion or exclusion, beyond knowledge or the unknown, beyond here and there or now and then. Thus, Bacon's text underscores the degree to which the disoriented interplay between apparent opposites that we find in the academy's vicinity furnishes the very conditions under which, ironically, academic orientation towards a future is attempted. Surviving the always-shifting institutional boundaries of enlightenment-censorship that seem to impel academic orientation, this interminable other 'without identity', constituted impossibly at the limits of the university, will return in the last section of this book.

Notes

1 Bill Readings, *The University in Ruins* (Cambridge, Mass., and London: Harvard University Press, 1996), p. 13. All further references will be given in the main body of the text.

2 Robert Young, 'The idea of a chrestomathic university', in *Logomachia: The Conflict of the Faculties*, ed. Richard Rand (Lincoln, NB and London: University of Nebraska Press, 1992), pp. 112–13. All further references will be given in the main body of the text.

3 Jean-Francois Lyotard, *The Postmodern Condition: A Report on Knowledge* (Manchester: Manchester University Press, 1984), pp. 4–5.

4 Jean-Francois Lyotard, *The Differend: Phrases in Dispute* (Minneapolis, MN: University of Minnesota Press, 1988).

5 Peggy Kamuf, *The Division of Literature, Or, The University in Deconstruction* (Chicago, IL: University of Chicago Press, 1997), p. 8. All further references will be given in the main body of the text.

6 See Young's 'The idea of a chrestomathic university', and also 'The dialectics of cultural criticism', *Angelaki*, 2:2 (1996) 9–24.

7 Kamuf quotes, and translates from, Hegel's *Werke* (Frankfurt: Suhrkamp, 1970), vol. 4, p. 316.

CHAPTER 4

Multiple submissions and little scrolls of parchment: censorship, knowledge and the academy

Some things I may tell you, which I
think you will not be unwilling to hear.

Francis Bacon, *New Atlantis*[1]

Literature and censorship

Reflecting a change of emphasis that is often taken to characterise the difference between 'progressive' academic professionals and institutions of the 1970s and 1980s and the 1990s, whereby radically optimistic oppositional politics have gradually been superseded by more subtly nuanced accounts of the various limitations and constraints placed upon the formation of literary and critical discourse, and how to work productively within them, a recent edition of *PMLA* was devoted to the special topic of Literature and Censorship.[2] In the introduction to this edition, Michael Holquist questions simple-minded notions of censorship as epitomising a struggle between opposed forced locked in a contest of wills. This vision of censorship, according to Holquist, rests on certain assumptions that have been problematised through and through from a multiplicity of theoretical perspectives. It necessitates a simplistic definition of the relationship between power and resistance as primarily one of absolute otherness and exclusion, when actually the 'fundamental quality of censorship' consists in the fact that 'its authority to prohibit can never be separated from its need to include',[3] or to regulate by way of strategies of engagement and negotiation with dissident voices; strategies which range from the appropriation and arbitration of available meanings, to anticipation – in a Bakhtinian sense – of otherness (and, in the context of self-censorship, anticipation of control) within social discourse. From this perspective, censorship can be conceptualised not simply in terms of repression, but can be seen more complexly as a crucial factor in the *production* of social (and academic) discourse and knowledge. Moreover, recognition of these fluid and shifting relationships between power and resistance, varying greatly within the 'myriad specific conditions' (p. 16) of censorship, undermines the essentialist totalisation of identities brought about by the simplistic disentanglement of 'Who–whom?' ('Who' does what to 'whom'?) that Holquist identifies as the 'traditional way to pose questions about censorship'.

Holquist goes on to suggest that, in any case, to posit essential freedoms prior to censorial restriction leaves us carrying the baggage of romantic notions of selfhood, agency, imagination and authentic voice, at the expense of contemporary understandings of language and identity as constituted in non-essentialist terms within 'external' dialogic space. The logical extension of this argument (one which seems progressive enough) is, of course, that all forms of social discourse and practice exceed the authority of the individual or of conscious intention. Holquist is quick to point out that the identification of authorship and the attempt to undertake biographical readings constitute a kind of censorial limiting of language, understood somewhat paradoxically as both impersonal and wantonly free. Indeed, despite Holquist's celebratory evocations of linguistic 'uncertainty', 'ambiguity' and 'slipperiness', causing loopholes and effects of 'interlinearity' that suggest new ways to theorise resistance to censorship, one suspects that the romantic ethos of subjectivity and freedom he eschews is being reconceptualised (and universalised) within the impersonal and indefinable identity of language itself, which seems to be understood very much in *a priori* terms. More important, however, the fact that Holquist's scepticism about essential freedoms within social discourse rests, at least in part, on a rebuttal of individual conscious intention as a prior and determining factor within the linguistic field enables him simultaneously to put the question of censorship in a way that seems rather to skirt around

the issue of responsibility. 'To be for or against censorship as such is
to assume a freedom no one has. Censorship *is*. One can only discriminate among its more and less repressive effects' (p. 16).

Censorship *is*. This linguistic formulation not only asserts
inevitability by claiming the preconditional existence of censorship.
It therefore also permits the attribution of an impersonal identity
(like language, though in different ways, censorship *is*) which constitutes censorship as of unimpeachable character. The theoreticist
claims of Holquist's introduction are not without their more immediate context. The editor's column of this edition of *PMLA*, 'On
multiple submissions',[4] attempts to justify the decision taken by the
journal's editorial board not to review articles that are under consideration by other journals. 'Does the policy constitute a kind of
censorship – the topic to which the current issue is devoted?' (p. 7)
asks Domna C. Stanton. Returning to Holquist's statement that
'Censorship *is*. One can only discriminate among its more and less
repressive effects', it is argued that the policy should not be viewed
in terms of an institutional mouthpiece wielding censorial power
against frenzied textual activity, prohibiting duplicate – and thereby
duplicitous – manuscripts, so as to achieve the 'order of discourse'
through orderly circulation. On the contrary, Stanton suggests that
the policy against multiple submissions adopted by several publica-
tions, not just *PMLA*, is intended to *improve* the treatment of
authors by journals generally, enabling the review process to be
expedited (fewer articles to be handled by editorial staff at any given
moment). Far from constituting repressive activity, such 'censorship'
therefore actually facilitates the process of bringing academic
discourse into the public domain, and as such might be considered
productive. In any case, censorship simply *is* (everyone else is doing
it, 'the majority of the journals [responding to a *PMLA* survey] instituted the policy in the 1980s' (p. 9)); and to level against *PMLA* a
charge of censorship, in the traditional sense of the suppression of
original material, would be nonsensical in the context of the present,
since 'the concept of an original typescript is meaningless in "the age
of mechanical reproduction"' (p. 8) (it is not just that everything is
done on computers, copied, faxed, e-mailed; nowadays nothing is
original anyway).

What is interesting about Stanton's defence of *PMLA*'s policy against multiple submissions is not simply that many of Holquist's theoreticist claims are taken up and used in the justification of one particular kind of censorship. More significantly, the process of censorship that Holquist describes from the vantage point of contemporary theoretical understandings can actually be seen to be underway in the editor's column itself. Stanton indeed regulates, by way of strategies of engagement and negotiation, the 'progressive' discourse of Holquist's article. Here are employed the whole range of tactics in relation to an essay (on censorship) which might otherwise embarrass editorial policy: appropriation, containment, arbitration of meaning, and even anticipation since, of course, the editorial precedes the introduction. Indeed, Holquist's notion that the 'authority to prohibit' can never be separated from 'the need to include' ironically typifies the Janus-faced nature of the editor's remarks: multiple submissions are prohibited, but nevertheless their authors, the constituency of *PMLA*, must be reassured, retained as members, included.

Having raised questions of the traces of dialogism and dialogic ambiguity constituted in, and constituting, any censored text, Holquist's article goes on to highlight in contrast the will-to-power pursued through the 'absence of interlinearity' (p. 21) dreamt of by the censor. Accordingly, the essay concludes by celebrating de Man's 'theory of reading'. Quoting de Man, Holquist writes: 'Because "negative knowledge about the reliability of linguistic utterances is made available" with particular force in literature, the kind of reading literature fosters may be "a powerful and indispensable tool in the unmasking of ideological aberrations"'.[5] Here, losing all sense of censorship as reading (aspiring to the 'absence of interlinearity', censorship promotes a kind of non-reading), Holquist attempts to separate censorship and reading as opposed activities. Thus, 'reading makes uneasy all proponents of certainty' (p. 22), that is proponents of censorship. Consequently, Holquist is keen to champion literature departments as potential spaces in which such 'reading', understood in relation to notions of polysemy, indeterminacy and ambivalence, might be undertaken. However, he goes on to claim that this would 'fulfill the function that Kant advocated for the philosophical faculty at Konigsberg: to serve as a protected zone in which propositions taught in other faculties as unquestionable truths could be freely interrogated' (p. 23). The very language used here is strikingly paradoxical. While literature departments are imagined as places in which to revel unreservedly in the riotous free-play of signifiers, they simultaneously serve – and can only function 'freely' – as 'protected zones', clearly marked off by impregnable boundaries of inclusion/exclusion. According to Holquist the pursuit of 'reading' along the lines de Man suggests enables literary critics to 'freely interrogate' (is this oxymoron intentional?) the 'propositions taught in other faculties'. Images of freedom through 'reading' therefore suddenly yield to the suggestion that literature departments serve as all-powerful censors and arbiters of 'other' sites of discourse, writing and knowledge. Here, de Man's 'theory of reading' is fashioned, paradoxically, as a space of isolation and entrapment: burdened with the responsibility of 'unmasking ideological aberrations' that are taken to permeate all other disciplines, literary critics become penned into the space of freedom by all the non-freedom around them! Holquist begins by suggesting that censorship constitutes a kind of reading ('censorship and translation are strategies to control meaning' (p. 18)), then tries to distinguish between the two, and finally comes to the shocking conclusion that 'reading' delimits a space from which to enact a kind of censorship.

Of course, this conclusion brings us right back to the editorial column, where 'the principal reason for adopting a policy against multiple submissions' is cited as 'the strain on ... referees' (p. 9). In this instance, reading is not an expression of freedom, it is a bind. The introduction of restrictions that might ease that bind, allowing readers greater freedom in their professional lives, is to be welcomed. Here we find in operation an inside/outside model structuring the terms of the multiple submissions debate, whereby 'Who–whom?', far from being rejected, is reconceptualised in terms of a split between, on the one hand, 'advisory committees' or 'editorial boards' made up of established and tenured academics and, on the other, aspiring authors, 'especially academics who are beginning their careers' (p. 8). This inside/outside model does more than to draw the boundaries, the limits, of reading. Since the 'outside' is also, in a sense, the 'inside' (submissions are only accepted from the membership of MLA), the debate itself points to the externalisation of an internal anxiety. Such projection of the 'inside' as an 'outside' is similarly manifest in Stanton's conclusion that 'market forces' are to blame for the crisis in academic 'writing practices' and the confusion of 'ethical codes' (p. 11). The 'market' is here presented as something that, except as an external menace, has little to do with *PMLA* or the institutions of criticism generally. This contradicts Bourdieu's contention in 'Censorship and the imposition of form' that, within the domain of specialised knowledges (or the academy), market conditions should be understood as 'the very structure of the field in which ... discourse is produced and circulated'.[6] Bourdieu argues that this 'structure of the field' places internal – and enabling – constraints on the very process of discursive production. For Bourdieu, it is this 'structure of the field' that constitutes censorship. Censorship is not something others do to us, but something we do to ourselves.

Ironically, Bourdieu's essay crops up in the notes to Holquist's introduction, as if the spectre of institutional self-censorship exists at the origins of how Holquist reads. (Indeed, Bourdieu's notion of academic discourse as 'a *compromise* between the *expressive interest* and a *censorship* constituted by the very structure of the field' is useful in mediating Holquist's concept of interlinearity, so as to avoid the trap of romanticising language in terms of some primordial, libidinous unity. It is, therefore, in Bourdieu's sense of an institutionalised field enabled by its own difference that I would wish to promote an understanding of interlinearity.) The spectre of such institutional self-censorship is important here, considering that Holquist's introduction, as well as making its own claims, produces potted readings of other articles comprising the volume, mirroring the strategies of engagement, negotiation and regulation of discourse found in the editor's column. (In a footnote, Stanton thanks Holquist for his 'exemplary help in coordinating the special topic' (p. 11).) It is also interesting that the editor, needing to 'include' as well as 'prohibit' the journal's readership, at one point passes off *PMLA* policy against multiple submissions as internal regulation or self-censorship (p. 7). This contradicts the externalisation of 'market forces' found elsewhere in the essay, and indicates the radically unstable nature of the inside/outside model which, as we have seen from Holquist's reference to Kant, structures the institution's thinking about itself. Here, despite firmly drawn boundaries of inclusion/exclusion, the 'inside' – the academy – itself comprises 'otherness' in the form of 'other faculties'. In the context of the *PMLA* number we have been discussing, this unstable oscillation between inside/outside, as an opposition which itself structures what can be said or thought about censorship, discourse and reading, freedom and limitation, production and repression, can only be partially contained and controlled by the various stratifications that take place within the issue, whereby constituencies in the debate are situated more or less 'inside' and 'outside' the project (for example, whereas Holquist's debt to Bourdieu is acknowledged, albeit in a note, Bourdieu is more or less excluded or repressed in the editor's appropriation of Holquist's insights). Rather, the internality of the 'outside' becomes everywhere apparent, so that the struggles between 'the membership', as the site of *production* and *reading*, and 'censorship', undertaken by *producers* of journals and *readers* or referees, can neither be understood as straightforwardly a matter of confrontation, nor headed off and stabilised within an ordering of discourse that seeks to repress the antagonistic *sameness* of these differences.[7]

Censorship and criticism

One of the places where questions of censorship have been raised most interestingly in recent times is Renaissance studies, which has itself been taken by many modern critics to provide a forum for larger arguments of contemporary relevance. In the concluding chapter to his book, *Licensed by Authority: Ben Jonson and the Discourses of Censorship*, Richard Burt brings his analysis into the present by tracing another (inadequately achieved) instance of the externalisation of internal institutional anxiety and crisis. Burt notes, particularly in debates about political correctness and the culture of educational institutions in the US, 'a formal symmetry in the rhetoric adopted by neoconservative critics and by the official defenders of the profession (for example, the executive council of the Modern Language Association)'.[8] 'Both sides,' according to Burt, 'say they are for diversity and open debate; both sides say they are telling the truth and accuse the other of engaging in scurrilous, irresponsible misrepresentation, fraud, distortion, and of attempting to censor or otherwise restrict authentic critical enquiry and genuine dialogue' (p. 161). During 1994, the year after Burt's book was published, MLA balloted its membership to endorse a resolution that condemned the Board of Trustees of Bennington College for the dismissal of 26 faculty members, the suggestion being that the right-wing Trustees had effectively 'censored' progressive research. Here, MLA members were reassuringly included by democratic means in the recognition of censorship taking place *elsewhere*. Paradoxically, however, they had been entreated to censure and to veto the Trustees of Bennington College for censorship! The internality of a threat that had been presented as somehow 'outside' the space of liberal critique was also tangible in the fact that censorship was perceived to have taken place *within* the institutions of higher education, or the academy, in the USA.

Yet this crisis of legitimation (and identity) has not been restricted to the institutions of criticism in the United States. Burt describes an 'ahistorical, moral definition of censorship' (censorship as a repressive, external threat to essential freedoms) that has been adopted by 'political critics' working in the early modern period (particularly British cultural materialists), which 'makes available in the Renaissance a certain essentially moral notion of critical opposition' (p. 152). 'By extension,' argues Burt, 'a similar kind of critical opposition becomes available in the present'. This is because, as I argued in Chapter 2, cultural materialism has displaced dialectical materialism, such that 'a form of reflection theory' has been reasserted, through which 'history has become a mirror in which contemporary political priorities have been substituted for the former certain ground of Marxist analysis', as Robert Young has noted.[9] By extension of his or her reading of the Renaissance in terms of 'moral' definitions of censorship, then, Burt contends that the political critic 'can be seen to oppose at once the professionalism and the formalism of a supposedly apolitical literary criticism and the postmodern (now post-Reaganite and post-Thatcherite) state. Thus censorship and criticism become self-identical terms that can be juxtaposed in a stable opposition; the critic is "opposed" to censorship' (pp. 152–3).

As we saw in Chapter 2, in order to carry out its political criticism, cultural materialism must oppose and expose reactionary standpoints on Renaissance literature and culture by showing them to be politically motivated, thus revealing their ostensible apoliticism as an ideological smokescreen. As the Foreword to *Political Shakespeare* puts it, cultural materialism 'does not, like much established literary criticism, attempt to mystify its perspective as the natural, obvious or right interpretation of an allegedly given textual fact'.[10] Yet to distinguish itself from these positions, political criticism has been forced to repeat the mystificatory stance of truth, reference and legality (we have noted the legalistic tone of 'allegedly') which it criticises in its opponents. Thus, in order to contest Nigel Lawson's conservative reading of *Troilus*, for example, Margot Heinemann, in her article included in the same volume, argues that the ex-Chancellor presents his quotations 'wholly out of dramatic context' which she then goes on properly to retrieve.[11] It will be recalled that this kind of manoeuvre in fact attempts to 'reground the link between representation and reference that has been questioned by the semiotics of the last twenty years', as Robert Young puts it.[12] Heinemann basically suggests that her position is more 'true' to its object than is Lawson's, and therefore effectively mystifies her reading as 'the right interpretation of an allegedly given textual fact'. Similarly, we have seen that Walter Cohen, in his essay 'Political criticism of Shakespeare', stresses the demythologising power of political criticism, but then becomes trapped in a position where he is compelled to insist that the left-wing 'partisanship' of contemporary 'political writing on Shakespeare' is 'not only compatible with but also necessary to a commitment to objectivity and scholarship'.[13] This in fact realigns radical critique with oppressive ideology, which tries to represent its politics, 'partisanship', as 'true'. Cohen's backsliding into 'objectivity and scholarship' signals at once a retreat from reactionary 'false politics' and a return to the politically disinterested, judicial image of the intellectual on which, according to cultural materialism, those politics are founded. It is indeed within the very process of differentiation that an identity emerges. Censorship (or right-wing 'misreading') and criticism]cannot be 'juxtaposed in a stable opposition', since political criticism can only legitimate and sustain itself as radically oppositional (or, as it were, 'free') by way of a forceful repression of its own 'politics' or, in other words, by censorship of itself.

Burt's *Licensed by Authority* argues against any clear-cut distinction between criticism and censorship, poetic liberty and licensed poetry, within the multiple and dispersed, and often equivocal and contradictory, spaces and conditions of the court and market during Jonson's time. Here, following Bourdieu's sense that the acquisition and formation of cultural capital (the market) depends on 'a *compromise* between the *expressive interest* and a *censorship* constituted by the very structure of the field in which discourse is produced', Burt argues that Renaissance panegyric 'involves neither willing submission to courtly tact nor open defiance of it but a mixture of both ... a neurotic compromise between the desire to fit in and the desire to express the censored material' (p. 11).

Such broadened and non-oppositional conceptions of censorship, in which the 'negative, repressive function is ... only one of the many regulatory mechanisms' (p. 13), and of criticism, which can be seen to legitimate as well as delegitimate both the writer and the court, are by no means exclusive to Burt's book. Richard Dutton's *Mastering the Revels*, for example, concludes that 'the position of the Master of the Revels, jealously protecting court privileges as much as he sought to suppress "dangerous matter", made him as much a friend of the actors as their overlord. The stability that his office gave to an exchange of meaning in the early modern theatrical market-place clearly played a part in fostering the unique vitality of the drama of the period'.[14] Annabel Patterson, writing as long ago as 1984, similarly emphasises this productive aspect of censorship, noting that 'it is to censorship that we in part owe our very concept of "literature"';[15] while others such as Janet Clare, Kevin Sharpe and Steven Mullaney have contributed to an ongoing and lively reconsideration of censorship and license within the field of Renaissance studies.[16] It would, of course, be misleading to suggest the emergence of a new consensus regarding these issues. Burt, for example, severely criticises Patterson for formulating a hermeneutics of censorship as coherent conscious strategy, and for retaining concepts of absolutist power and tyrannical prohibition in the Renaissance which effectively rule out a critique of 'the present liberal modern state' (p. 155). Here, again, the unenlightened 'other' (Patterson) is both contained and prohibited within the space of 'progressive' criticism (Burt), this kind of 'censoring' being a condition of its more 'radical' workings. It is therefore not my aim to attempt to negotiate and resolve (i.e. to censor) the differences between critics, so as to achieve the order of this 'buzzing of discourse'. Rather, I want to contribute to the debate – and perhaps reflect on it more widely – by coming again at questions of censorship and criticism, prohibition and knowledge, freedom and limitation, writing and reading, in the context of the institutional space of the academy itself; this time, at a crucial moment in its development, in the early modern past. To do this, I will undertake a 'reading' (though the text itself problematises this activity) of Bacon's *New Atlantis*.

In light of the contemporary concerns that have gone before, such a reading inevitably begs the question of historical difference and relationship. While I am concerned not to repeat the kind of 'reflectionism' that Robert Young associates with cultural materialist strategies of reading, whereby the past functions rather straightforwardly as a platform for larger arguments of topical relevance, nevertheless it seems to me equally problematic to position *New Atlantis* historically according to crude notions of epoch or chronological pastness, since such ostensibly stable conceptions of time (and indeed place) are themselves rendered uncertain in the text by the *uncanny* relation of Bensalem to Europe and, by extension, to Enlightenment values of progress and linearity. This uncanny relationship upsets the designation of a self-identical point of origin or ground on which rest traditional notions of historical time and historical difference (themselves allied to those Enlightenment values). However, *New Atlantis* may be of interest to the late twentieth-century reader in that it seems possible to locate Bacon's text within the interstitial space of a shift from 'premodern' to 'modern' types of legitimation, one that Lyotard discusses extensively in his account of the postmodern condition. In *Lyotard: Writing the Event*, Geoffrey Bennington states that 'Lyotard suggests a change from a sort of classical and premodern science which produced narratives for seeking legitimisation in an origin or ground, a first principle or a transcendental authority, to 'modern' forms of legitimation based on consensus... [this] type of legitimation allows for the possibility that the discussion of experts can lead to an improvement in the rules for speaking truth, and that this improvement can be projected into a future under the sign of progress'.[17] This transitional phase resonates with the shift from deduction to induction, from similitude to Cartesian separation and classification, from sameness to difference, that can be located at the horizon of the early modern period and, more particularly, identified with Bacon himself. Reading (and locating historically) New Atlantis in the interstices of these forms of legitimation, in a space of contestation and struggle between the authority of a ground and the concerns of the present with its politics of future use-value, it is not surprising that the text itself raises questions of historical method, taking us beyond simple 'either/or' choices of sameness/difference.

Seeing censorship as a constitutive feature of emergent 'modern' forms of legitimation, my reading of New Atlantis will necessarily place an emphasis on the productive or enabling role that censorship has in the formation of knowledge. This may seem to lead ultimately to a rather benign view of censorship itself, in line with the reformulation by PMLA that I began by looking at so critically. However, it seems to me that any departure from a notion of censorship as 'bad' is troubling to the modern liberal mind mainly because it destabilises an oppositional logic which identifies knowledge as 'good'. The pros and cons of PMLA's policy against multiple submissions were debated hotly and at some length in letters by various members which the journal published in its Forum during 1994 and 1995. Yet the very fact that this space of engagement and negotiation was held open stole the thunder of more dissident voices against PMLA 'censorship' (along the lines of 'we must be liberal to publish this') and thus – within the very space and activity of progressive discourse – enacted a kind of censorship of criticism. In other words, censorship existed here as 'the very structure of the field' in which liberal discussion and radical critique was able to take place. Yet this recognition does not so much produce a view of censorship as after all 'not bad', as prompts us to reconsider conceptions of enlightened academic discourse and its particular formations of knowledge as, in contrast, 'good'. It is in the spirit of this different approach to the non-oppositional relation of censorship and knowledge that I will read New Atlantis.

Enlightenment and secrecy

According to Rawley, Bacon's secretary, the 'fable' of *New Atlantis* was devised by its author so as to 'exhibit therein a model or description of a college instituted for the interpreting of nature and the producing of great and marvellous works for the benefit of men, under the name of Salomon's House'.[18] Salomon's House exemplifies in ideal terms the advancement of learning, in the context both of academic principle and institutional practice. As B. H. G. Wormald has put it, as well as providing 'a framework of directing axioms conducive to learning's advancement', *New Atlantis* is Bacon's 'vision of an institution established by government for furthering natural philosophy/science'.[19] As a source of enlightenment, discovery and invention, Salomon's House is, to borrow Burt's phrase, licensed by authority: it is created and officially sanctioned by royal act (p. 58); and the Father of Salomon's House, who imparts to the European visitors 'the true state' – the foundations, instruments, functions and ordinances – of the institution, is himself described as arriving, almost regally, 'in state' (p. 69). The close connections between the state and the academy are underlined, then, through reference to the authority of the House of Salomon's officials; but also the authority of the institution is reflected in the orderliness that everywhere characterises its activities. As a research institute, it supports the study of, among other things, the natural sciences, mathematics and geometry, philosophy, medicine, the mechanical arts, and optics and acoustics. The description offered by the Father of the means and ends of these pursuits is given in terms of an extremely lengthy and well-ordered identificatory and classificatory grouping and listing of the various faculties and functions within the academy, bordering on the facile, so that the almost legalistic monologism of the Father's speech can be taken to reflect the legality as well as the orderliness of the institution. Indeed, since it tells us so little that might really be interesting (about scientific ethics, for example, or the precise terms of the relationship between state and academy) the Father's account of the 'true state' of Salomon's House is characterised by an 'absence of interlinearity' to which, according to Holquist, all censors aspire, alerting us to the possibility that the revelation to which we are brought in the concluding section of *New Atlantis* may be communicated in the very language of censorship.

The orderliness of the institution's academic disciplines is matched by that of the conduct of its officials. As Robert K. Faulkner notes, in *Francis Bacon and the Project of Progress*, 'every official performs his function ... everyone does what he is ordered'.[20] However, as Faulkner points out, 'All this order is the more remarkable since the relation of king, city, nation, state, and scientist is not clarified. The order that orders ... is hidden'. It is generally recognised that this Utopian domain of enlightened knowledge, declaring itself dedicated to '*Light*: to have *light*' (p. 59), is founded upon such concealment, although critics disagree as to exactly what is being concealed. Jerry Weinberger notes that Bensalemite 'science is shrouded in secrecy, denying the possibility of full enlightenment', and he attributes this to Bacon's sense that 'the politics of science must be secret and retired because only the most resolute souls will be willing to embrace such a world with full knowledge of its moral risks and dangers'.[21] In other words, any consideration of the ethical implications and responsibilities of science and learning must be censored in order for enlightenment, advancement and progress to continue apace. In contrast, Faulkner reads *New Atlantis* in the context of what he sees as Bacon's belief that the 'science of government is a thing secret and reserved, to be handled with reverence and even in silence' (p. 235). According to this analysis, it is the governing social and material contexts and conditions rather than the moral implications of the academy's activities that must remain invisible: a different sort of politics of science. This is backed up by Faulkner's contention that the very processes of production underlying the achievements of Salomon's House and Bensalem generally are concealed. He states, 'we are plied with a promise of pleasant affluence, but any system of painful industry and production is kept well behind the scenes' (p. 246). Indeed, the catalogue offered by the Father of Salomon's House of its faculties and functions barely touches upon the labours of production involved (we are occasionally told *what* is done, but rarely *how* it is done), so that science and knowledge are described, as it were, within the rhetorical terms of commodity fetishism, in which the means to the end are hidden from view.

This difficulty of saying exactly what is concealed in *New Atlantis*, either at the social or textual level, arises partly out of the problem of identifying something that is not, in any apparent way, there. Absence can, of course, be defined simply in an oppositional relationship to presence, but (as we shall see in *New Atlantis*) what is present is itself a matter of interpretation or reading, and as such cross-cut by effects of 'uncertainty', 'ambiguity' or 'slipperiness' of the kind described by Holquist. Thus, the identificatory strategies of an oppositional logic of presence/absence are undermined by the 'otherness' or internal difference of what is present. Indeed, Bensalem, as both an exemplary 'model' and a 'secret conclave' (p. 51) exists, in Freudian terms, in an *uncanny* relation to the positivistic knowledge, progress and plenitude of the nascent European-Enlightenment project, representing simultaneously 'what is familiar and agreeable' and 'what is concealed and kept out of sight'.[22] In these terms, the polarities and boundaries of known/unknown, visible/invisible, inside/outside collapse into more complex and undecidable formations epitomised by the non-self-identical doubleness of Europe/Bensalem. *New Atlantis* is, complexly, both a beacon of previously undiscovered wisdom and truth and, as Bacon puts it, 'a mirror in the world worthy to hold men's eyes' (p. 60): both subject and object, self and other.

Thus, it would seem that critics and readers of *New Atlantis* are placed in the same boat as the European visitors themselves. That is, these critics become, as it were, knowledgeably ignorant, just as the European voyagers become, as it were, ignorantly knowledgeable, of Bensalemite learning and society. The journey of the Europeans towards revelation, like that of the critic towards understanding, is beset at every turn – even, as we have seen, at the end – by limitations, confinements and prohibitions, as if such constraints were less an obstacle to than a *condition* of enlightenment. A host of terms are laid down before the strangers can come ashore, including the restriction of numbers allowed to enter Bensalem, and the taking of an oath prior to the 'license to come on land' (p. 40). They are 'sent to, and brought to the Stranger's House' (p. 41) or, in other words, escorted along predetermined routes. They are subjected to an initial period of quarantine in 'chambers' and 'cells' in which are continually present 'six people appointed to attend you, for any business you may have abroad' (p. 42). Whether or not these officials are intermediaries or guards, their job is clearly to prevent forcibly contaminatory contact between the Bensalemites and the Europeans. Here, again, we find that the Utopian space of enlightenment is a 'protected zone', quick to enforce its borders against real and symbolic threats of infection. However, the brick walls that keep the strangers *in* are also presented as a means of ensuring undisturbed freedom. They are assured, 'do not think yourselves restrained, but rather left to your rest and ease' (p. 42), and subsequently spend 'three days joyfully and without care' (p. 44). In this sense, the boundary which materially divides the Europeans and the Bensalemites is itself symbolically subverted and transgressed the moment it is enforced, since the freedoms of both are guaranteed by the prohibitory borders of both, opening out the suggestion of an identity or parallel state which contradicts images of hermetically closed non-contact and difference.

It is worth looking more closely at ways in which the enlightenment offered by the Bensalemites is, as Weinberger puts it, 'shrouded in secrecy'. Revelation is made in the rather conspiratorial manner of exclusive, private conversations. The officer of Salomon's House encountered initially by the Europeans desires, we are told, 'to speak with some few of us, whereupon only six of us stayed, and the rest avoided the room' (p. 44). The interview with the Father of Salomon's House is described in terms of 'private access' and 'private conference with one that ye shall choose'; and, prior to his disclosure, all other company departs and even the pages are 'warned' from the room (pp. 70–1). Moreover, the special privilege of revealed wisdom is highlighted by reference to 'the laws of secrecy which we have for our travellers' (p. 46) and through the affirmation that Bensalem is founded on 'fundamental laws' comprising 'interdicts and prohibitions which we have touching the entrance of strangers'. Furthermore, just as things start to get interesting, the speaker is invariably called away rather abruptly by a mysterious messenger (pp. 49, 68). Some critics have interpreted these interruptions as evidence of Bensalemite surveillance and self-censorship,[23] yet they do not seem to inhibit, at a later stage, further scenes of revelation which dynamise and propel the structure of the narrative itself. Flying in the face of critical assertions that Bensalemite secrecy masks the organising principles and infrastructural pith of their soci-ety, these shenanigans (the orchestration of private conversations, the sense of exclusive revelation, even of clandestine liaison) might therefore appear to be little more than an elaborate way of convinc-ing the strangers that Bensalemites have juicy secrets to share! From this point of view, Bensalemite secrecy does not constitute a form of repression operating at the threshold of enlightenment, but enacts a kind of productive censorship, in which the controlled management and manipulation of what is apparently unsaid and unrevealed lends meaning, value and authority to what *is* said and discovered. Correspondingly, from this perspective, we move from Faulkner's contention that 'the order that orders ... is hidden' (repression) to Lyotard's 'problematic of legitimation' of modern science, in which the non-transcendental legality of the law problematises dreams of unearthing ultimate proofs of prior truths, but also prompts Enlightenment fantasies of improvement, development, progress, under the sign of a future (production).[24]

On beginning the instruction of the strangers, the officer of Salomon's House states that there are 'some things I may tell you, which I think you will not be unwilling to hear' (p. 44). The com-mencement of Bensalemite disclosure is couched in delightfully interlinear terms: reading between the lines, the implication is, of course, that there are other things that may not be told, and which in any case the Europeans would be unwilling to hear. Weinberger argues that the subject of this 'unsaid' is itself prohibitory restraint: 'if Bensalemite law and policy are consistent, strangers unwilling to stay, or those judged unfit to stay, must have been restrained by force or killed. This doubtless the sailors would not have been will-ing to hear'.[25] However, the idea that the officer's speech censors (or is censored) is not, in Holquist's terms at least, consistent with the interlinearity of the phrasing found here. The sophisticated twists and turns of syntax produce, as de Man puts it, 'negative knowledge about the reliability of linguistic utterances', encouraging precisely the kind of probing and insightful reading advocated by Holquist as the very basis on which literature departments and the academy gen-erally might function progressively. Thus, the censorship found by Weinberger in the official's statement actually produces a kind of enlightenment. Although it is possible to read into the official's remarks a sinister and foreboding sense of limitation, we can also interpret what he says as an act of enticement rather than prohibition – though no less disingenuous, perhaps – urging the listener to believe that there is more to know beyond the threshold of what is said, and thus sustaining the very project of enlightenment.

At another point, the officer says 'because he that knoweth least is fittest to ask questions, it is more reason, for the entertainment of the time, that ye ask me questions, than that I ask you' (p. 46). This proposition might immediately raise suspicion: 'ask me anything you like' is not the same as 'I will tell you everything I know'. Indeed, granting the freedom to ask ingeniously shifts the onus from the expert official to the unknowledgeable questioner, to the extent that it may be seen to provide an ideal opportunity to neglect a mass of information. This leaves the Europeans no grounds for complaint about suppression since no prior limitations have been placed on the questioning. Yet it is precisely the absence of these limitations, in the sense of a fixed context of discussion, that limits what will become known. Reading between the lines, it seems that – within the particular formation of enlightenment found here – limits and parameters are an essential precondition if knowledge is to be optimised. From another perspective, the idea of an almost bottomless pit of hitherto undiscovered knowledge responsive to any question whatsoever (although attainable only by the fixing of contextualising limits) encourages the unknown to be sifted *ad infinitum*; so that once again it is indispensably within the context of boundaries (known/unknown, visible/invisible, inside/outside), albeit the crossing and relocating of them, that we find the enabling conditions of the enlightenment project.

Poetic vision

The problem of enlightenment in *New Atlantis* rests, then, on whether truth is or can be divined in a prior relation to knowledge, or whether knowledge – as a complex formation of linguistic encounters and propositions – represents truth into being. We are told early on that Bensalem has been founded on Christian revelation. A mile out to sea, a 'great pillar of light' topped by a 'large cross of light' appears 'about twenty years after the ascension of our

Saviour' to the 'people of the city'. For a while, this revelation remains shrouded in mystery, as the sign conveys no message as such. However, one of the wise men of the society of Salomon's House is at hand and, 'having awhile attentively and devoutly viewed and contemplated the pillar and cross', he prays to God that interpretation be forthcoming. While all others remain miraculously transfixed, the wise man alone is permitted to approach the pillar of light, and delivered to him is an 'arc or chest' in which is found a 'book' containing 'all the canonical books of the Old and New Testament' as well as a 'Letter' bringing the good news of salvation from St. Bartholomew (pp. 47–8). This scene lies at the origins of a symbolic interplay which runs throughout *New Atlantis*, between the spiritual 'light' of Christianity and the project of enlightenment founded by the House of Salomon, suggesting that its advancement of learning is divinely sanctioned and illuminates a transcendental signified. Thus, unsurprisingly, the wondrous meaning of the 'great pillar of light' becomes apparent foremost to the 'house or college' (in the shape of the representative figure of the wise man) which is 'the very eye of this kingdom' (p. 48).

However, the relation between Christian 'light' and scientific enlightenment becomes problematic at the very moment the analogy between the two hardens. A few pages later, we are told that Salomon's House is itself the 'lanthorn' or light of Bensalem (p. 58). It is not simply that this doubling and displacement of the source of illumination might appear heretical. More importantly, the 'eye' that sees is itself the 'light' that illuminates. Christopher Pye has described as the 'Renaissance theory of sight beams'[26] the concept that the eye is the *agent* of what it perceives, and indeed in the pageant poetry written to celebrate James I's accession, the king himself is represented simultaneously as the ultimate source of light, a sun, and a self-illuminating, all-seeing eye.[27] The currency of such contemporary ideas can be traced elsewhere in *New Atlantis*. Although we are told that Bensalem is a copious source of 'light', it remains 'hidden and unseen to others', while the less enlightened Old World is nevertheless 'open and in a light' to Bensalemite travellers (p. 51). This apparent reversal of the scenes of illumination and darkness in fact attributes the presence or absence of 'light' to the subject rather than the object, the seeing eye rather than the thing viewed. Such configurations seem to align more with Bacon's views on poetry than with his views on science. Quoting from *The Advancement of Learning*, Faulkner states: 'According to Bacon ... poetry is ... a rational management of invented illusion to help satisfy real desire. Poets do not divine an ideal or feel the sublime. They incline to "submit the shows of things to the desires of the mind"' (p. 237). The emphasis within Bacon's concept of poetic vision on subjectivity and sense-impression clearly foreshadows certain strands of eighteenth-century philosophical discourse, but most interestingly this view of poetry as the conscious manipulation of consciousness advocates rationalism without recourse to pre-existing 'truth'. Poetry's self-reflexivity seems, however, to be present in Bensalemite science: Salomon's House is both the eye that sees and the light that illuminates. Indeed, it is possible to reread the scene of Christian revelation in *New Atlantis* in light of Bacon's conception of poetic vision: that is, in aligning Christianity and science as compatible belief systems or narratives and thus satisfying spiritual and secular needs simultaneously, the spectacle serves to 'submit the shows of things to the desires of the mind'. Thus, Faulkner casts doubt on the miraculous pillar of light, drawing attention to the theatrical staginess of the scene of revelation (we are told 'the boats stood all as in a theatre' (p. 47)), and noting, in the Father's description of Salomon's House, 'the scientist's ability "to represent all manner of reflections, refractions, and multiplications of visual beams of objects," and to represent also all manner of "false apparitions, impostures and illusions"' (p. 243). Indeed, the Father reveals that the Bensalemite science of optics has enabled its proponents to produce artificially 'all delusions and deceits of the sight in figures' as well as unnaturally vivid views of 'objects far off; as in the heaven and remote places'. 'We make artificial rain-bows, halos, and circles of light,' he goes on, before concluding with a description of the 'houses of deceits of the senses' within Salomon's House itself (pp. 78–80). We can only conclude from this irony that, as Faulkner puts it, 'Bacon thinks divinations but artificial light, imaginings like all suppositions of divinity' (p. 239). Thus, it is not that Salomon's House provides an exemplary, model college in which natural or divine phenomena might be discovered and exhibited; rather, revelation is, in Bourdieu's terms, 'the very structure of the field' in which the 'rational management of invented illusion' can take place so as to 'satisfy real desire', either that of the Bensalemites or the Europeans. And, of course, 'the very structure of the field in which discourse is produced and circulated' constitutes Bourdieu's definition of censorship. Here, however, we are alerted by the fact that it simultaneously constitutes a definition of enlightenment.

Writing and the academy

Since divination in fact represents the 'rational management of invented illusion', it follows that censorship, as the 'structure of the field' in which it takes place, is enacted non-repressively, as it were, on disclosures that have no primordial unity or transcendental grounding. The revelation of the 'Book' that accompanies the miraculous 'light' of Christianity is, however, presented as being instantaneously and transcendentally complete. It contains not only the portions of the Bible written by 20 AD but also 'some other books which were not at that time written', yet which are 'nevertheless in the Book' (p. 49). In Faulkner's terms, the productive process – the labour and temporality of writing – once again appears to have been concealed or repressed, within the fetishised spectacle of a spontaneous text, both unique and fully finished. From this kind of perspective, the wholeness of the Book is itself a product of repressive exclusions.

As if to confirm the unity of the Book, its reception is characterised by the absence of interlinearity, since by 'a great miracle' similar to 'that of the Apostles in the original Gift of Tongues' the various peoples of Bensalem – 'Hebrews, Persians and Indians, besides the natives' – are all able to read the Book and Letter 'as if they had been written in his own language' (p. 49). This constitutes a kind of reverse Babel effect in which cultural, religious and linguistic fragmentation is miraculously overcome and restored within a monological moment of absolute certainty and harmony. What would appear to be a reclamation of a prior wholeness, both of the text and of the people, is achieved, then, at the expense of any slippage between the lines. Translational ambiguity is entirely dispensed with: just as the productive processes of writing are omitted, so the labour of translation is also redundant and, indeed, even the effort of reading seems to be discounted, since the meaning of the text becomes instantly and unequivocally apparent to all present. This absence of interlinearity suggests, once again, a definition of censorship. But here we find censorship – within the terms of a repressive hypothesis, the harbinger of violence and danger to the project of enlightenment – (co)operating at the very moment of overcoming a castrating severance or fragmentation of the Word and the Nation. The damage done to the repressive hypothesis by this paradoxical state of affairs is compounded, since such censorship cannot be said to excise or suppress an earlier or more complete original: the Book we are dealing with is the ultimate prior text, or otherwise it is part of the 'invented illusion' brought into being by the event itself. Here, denied the lag or gap that it requires between a primary and secondary 'object', the theory of repression runs into trouble: the originality of the Book, its unfaltering continuity with the moment, its non-concealment of anything, is indisputable either way and yet, paradoxically, it is subjected to a kind of censorship. This forces us once again to rethink conventional notions of censorship as blemish, and therefore, by extension, paradoxically unsettles an oppositional image of knowledge as purity at the very moment it would seem, superficially at least, to confirm it.

Both the text and the society of *New Atlantis* seem to revolve around the production and circulation of 'little scrolls of parchment' which, embodying the authority of the Christian-Bensalemite order, continually reinvoke the scene of revelation of the Book and the Letter. On their first encounter with the Bensalemites, the Europeans are not spoken to, but read to from such a scroll, 'written in Hebrew, and in ancient Greek, and in good Latin of the School' (p. 38); that is, in universally legible language, not unlike the miraculous Book itself. However, the scroll welcomes or 'includes' only to 'prohibit' and exclude its audience: 'Land ye not, none of you', it commands. Content and context are here antagonistically fused, as the prohibitory message is delivered within an enticing gesture of openness, greeting, legibility. A similar scroll of 'shining yellow parchment' is indispensable within the ritual of the Tirsan feast, given to honour the Father of the family who can boast 'thirty persons descended of his body alive together' (p. 60). This scroll is the King's Charter, containing 'gift of revenew, and many privileges, exemptions and points of honour' (pp. 60–2). The scroll thus simultaneously rewards and regulates generation, since breeding, it is suggested, is mainly a means to achieve financial security: thus, those that marry for 'alliance, or portion' (dowry) are 'almost indifferent ... of issue' (p. 67). By conferring large amounts of money on the family as a whole, the scroll effectively limits what it celebrates, ingeniously controlling at the same time as glorifying population, and in the process offering freedoms to its beneficiaries which turn out, simultaneously, to be restrictions. Similarly, when the Father of Salomon's House conveys to the unnamed narrator of *New Atlantis* the substance of the final portions of the text, he does so with his blessing and largess, giving 'leave to publish it' as well as 'about two thousand ducats, for a bounty' (p. 83). If such plenitude is intended to signal the ripe finishedness and full presence of the text, then nevertheless we have already seen how the monologic purity of the Father's descriptions contains, as a precondition, a host of limitations, restrictions and prohibitions. As I have suggested, these serve not so much to conceal an 'inner' truth, as critics of *New Atlantis* would have it, as to suggest unfinishedness, more to know. From this perspective, a finished text would seem to be wholly dependent on its unfinishedness, perhaps offering a key to the question of why Rawley inscribes at the end of *New Atlantis* '[THE REST WAS NOT PERFECTED]' (p. 83), even though, as Faulkner points out, Bacon must have considered it ready for publication to have translated it into Latin, the universal language (the language of the book), before his death (Faulkner, p. 321).[28]

Thus, in the context of the institutionalisation and systematised circulation of writing underlined here by the powerful ties between academy and state found in Bensalem, these examples show once more how openness, freedom from obligation, and textual originality remain inseparable from forms of censorship, regulation and restraint that produce them. This paradox of writing in the public domain returns us to the terms of the multiple submissions debate, which is itself indicative of various anxieties within the culture of academic institutions today. It is therefore possible to argue the contemporary relevance of *New Atlantis* in terms of its suggestion that, from the outset, the borders between freedom and prohibition, knowledge and censorship, inside and outside, are radically unstable within the space and vision of the institution, collapsing these supposed oppositions into more complex and indeterminate formations characterised by, for example, the non-self-identical doubleness, the uncanny twinning, of Europe/Bensalem, or the antagonistic *sameness* of producers/referees of journals and their membership. However, in relation to questions of the limitations placed on the production of knowledge within the academy, it is also suggested that, while such boundaries can never seem to be stabilised, their very indeterminacy and fluidity is precisely what sustains the enlightenment project. The masquerade of secrecy in Bensalem achieves this canny effect: no matter how far the frontiers of knowledge are pushed back, there's always more to know just over the threshold. As we have seen, then, it is the absence of limitations that limit what can become 'known', while the positioning of boundaries, particularly shifting and thus incessant ones, remains vital in the crossing or journey towards enlightenment. It is not so surprising that, faced with submissions that seem boundless in more ways than one, institutional bodies like *PMLA* should redraw boundaries that at the same time ever recede,[29] such as those that simultaneously 'prohibit' and 'include', to protect and prolong the dream of progress and even, paradoxically, progressive research. *New Atlantis* forces a reconsideration of the boundaries of the academy in the modern context, suggesting that the instability of institutional limits may be longstanding and functional (by which I do not mean 'good') rather than symptomatic of a sudden crisis, a new moment of breakdown. This recognition by no means rehabilitates in any fatalistic way the values of Enlightenment, but on the contrary suggests that we need to think differently about the conditions of censorship and knowledge in order to shake their grip.

Notes

1 Francis Bacon, *New Atlantis and The Great Instauration*, ed. Jerry Weinberger (Illinois: Harlan Davidson, 1989), p. 44.
2 *PMLA*, 109:1 (January 1994), Special Topic: Literature and Censorship.
3 Michael Holquist, 'Corrupt originals: the paradox of censorship', *PMLA*, 109:1 (January 1994) 14–25, p. 14. All further references will be given in the main body of the text.

4 Domna C. Stanton, 'Editor's column, on multiple submissions', *PMLA* 109.1 (January 1994) 7–13. All further references will be given in the main body of the text.

5 Michael Holquist, 'Corrupt originals', p. 21, quoted from de Man, 'The resistance to theory', in his *The Resistance to Theory* (Minneapolis, MN: University of Minnesota Press, 1986), pp. 10–11.

6 Pierre Bourdieu, 'Censorship and the imposition of form', in *Language and Symbolic Power*, ed. and intr. John B. Thompson, trans. Gino Raymond and Matthew Adamson (Oxford: Basil Blackwell, 1991), p. 137.

7 Aside from the fact that *PMLA* will only consider contributions from members of the Modern Language Association (my membership has lapsed) that have not been submitted elsewhere, it is interesting to wonder what kind of dilemma would be posed by submission of this essay. Non-publication could, of course, be construed in a straightforward way as suppression of criticism levelled against the policy on multiple submissions. But publication could also be seen, in my chapter's own terms, as a tactical engagement and negotiation with critical discourse, a gesture of openness and liberalism which would pre-empt the critical force of the essay (though at the same time corroborating some of its claims). Such a response would in a very real sense 'prohibit' critique by inclusion: precisely Holquist's definition of censorship.

8 Richard Burt, *Licensed by Authority: Ben Jonson and the Discourses of Censorship* (Ithaca and London: Cornell University Press, 1993), p. 161. All further references will be given in the main body of the text.

9 Robert Young, *White Mythologies: Writing, History and the West* (London: Routledge, 1990), p. 89.

10 Jonathan Dollimore and Alan Sinfield, Foreword, in *Political Shakespeare: New Essays in Cultural Materialism*, ed. Jonathan Dollimore and Alan Sinfield (Manchester: Manchester University Press, 1985), p. viii.

11 Margot Heinemann, 'How Brecht read Shakespeare', in *Political Shakespeare*, ed. Jonathan Dollimore and Alan Sinfield, p. 203.

12 Robert Young, 'The politics of "the politics of literary theory"', *Oxford Literary Review*, 10 (1988) 131–57, p. 132.

13 Walter Cohen, 'Political criticism of Shakespeare', in *Shakespeare Reproduced: the Text in History and Ideology*, ed. Jean Howard and Marion O' Connor (London: Methuen, 1987), p. 20.

14 Richard Dutton, *Mastering the Revels: The Regulation and Censorship of English Renaissance Drama* (London: Macmillan, 1991), p. 248.

15 Annabel Patterson, *Censorship and Interpretation: The Conditions of Writing and Reading in Early Modern England* (Madison, WN: University of Wisconsin Press, 1984), p. 4.

16 Janet Clare, *Art Made Tongue-Tied by Authority: Elizabethan and Jacobean Censorship* (Manchester: Manchester University Press, 1990);

Kevin Sharpe, *Criticism and Compliment: The Politics of Literature in the England of Charles I* (Cambridge: Cambridge University Press, 1987); Steven Mullaney, *The Place of the Stage: License, Play and Power in Renaissance England* (Chicago, IL: University of Chicago Press, 1987).

17 Geoffrey Bennington, *Lyotard: Writing the Event* (Manchester: Manchester University Press, 1988), p. 115.

18 Francis Bacon, *New Atlantis and The Great Instauration*, ed. Jerry Weinberger, p. 36. All further references will be given in the main body of the text.

19 B. H. G. Wormald, *Francis Bacon: History, Politics and Science, 1561–1626* (Cambridge: Cambridge University Press, 1993), p. 235.

20 Robert K. Faulkner, *Francis Bacon and the Project of Progress* (Maryland: Rowman and Littlefield, 1993), p. 248. All further references will be given in the main body of the text.

21 Jerry Weinberger, Introduction to *New Atlantis and The Great Instauration*, p. xxxii.

22 Sigmund Freud, 'The uncanny', *The Penguin Freud Library Volume 14: Art and Literature* (London: Penguin, 1985), p. 345.

23 Faulkner, for example, notes that the officer of Salomon's House 'waxes enthusiastic and didactic about Bensalem's salvation from infidelity, through the "apostolical and miraculous evangelism of St. Bartholomew." A messenger interrupts him when he pauses. When he returns, the topic is the marvel of Bensalem as unknown knower, and our governor-priest smiles at the suggestion that Bensalem benefits from supernatural spirits. Does someone listen and direct from behind the scenes?' (pp. 245–6). Later on, Faulkner remarks that 'the priest is interrupted by a messenger just after he waxes evangelical, and is called away; we are later told of devices for transmitting sounds in pipes and lines' (p. 249).

24 Jean-François Lyotard, in *The Postmodern Condition*, writes: 'Scientific knowledge cannot know and make known that it is the true knowledge without resorting to the other, narrative, kind of knowledge, which from its point of view is no knowledge at all. Without such recourse it would be in the position of presupposing its own validity and would be stooping to what it condemns: begging the question, proceeding on prejudice' (*The Postmodern Condition* (Manchester: Manchester University Press, 1984), p. 29). Yet it is in relation to this passage that Bennington, in *Lyotard: Writing the Event*, discusses Lyotard's concept of a shift from premodern to modern forms of scientific legitimation which allow for consensual discussion among experts leading to improvements in the rules for speaking the truth, 'projected into a future under the sign of progress' (p. 115).

25 Jerry Weinberger, Introduction to *New Atlantis and The Great Instauration*, p. xvi.

26 Christopher Pye, 'The sovereign, the theater, and the kingdome of

darknesse: Hobbes and the spectacle of power', in *Representing the English Renaissance*, ed. Stephen Greenblatt (California: University of California Press, 1988), p. 295.

27 Pye's article touches upon the solar imagery of early modern power, but for a fuller discussion of this in relation to the literature of James I's accession, see my 'Sovereign counterfeits: the trial of the pyx', *Renaissance Quarterly*, 49:2 (Summer 1996) 334–59.

28 *New Atlantis* is indeed open-ended and, as it were, unfinished at both ends, since the text commences by joining the Europeans in mid-voyage. Kate Aughterson, in '"The Waking Vision": reference in the *New Atlantis*', *Renaissance Quarterly*, 45:1 (Spring 1992) 119–39, argues that the opening passage, beginning, 'We sailed from Peru, (where we had continued by the space of one whole year)', comprises 'simple vocabulary', 'accurate geographical directions' and a straightforward fit between syntactic and temporal sequence, which epitomises an 'apparently closed system of determining referents' (p. 122). Aughterson thereby suggests that, apparently, 'no reference is unfixed or floating', yet the irony of this metaphorical representation of reference as 'unfloating' is that the opening sequence of *New Atlantis* is about a voyage at sea! Moreover, the description of the Europeans as having 'continued' awhile in Peru carries the sense of ongoingness, impermanence, flux. Thus, Aughterson concludes that 'metaphoric "open-endedness"' arises out of the seemingly 'closed system': to some extent, this parallels my argument about the inseparable relation of censorship and freedom or enlightenment in *New Atlantis*.

29 In regard to the almost vanishing boundaries or horizons of the enlightenment project, it is interesting that Richard Burt in *Licensed by Authority* predicates his analysis and methodology on the abandonment of 'the notion of the absolute priority of a given determination or horizon' (p. 23). Thus, in relation to the licensing and censorship of the theatre, 'no final horizon can rightly be said to operate consistently at all points as the determining constraint' (p. 22). Burt describes his critical strategies as 'Foucauldian, post-Marxist', and thereby invokes, within his theorisation of censorship, 'multiplicity ... decentred subjectivity, textual heterogeneity, indeterminacy, polysemy, and so on': the list itself, unfinished and ongoing, journeys towards an almost vanishing horizon! Although he is sceptical of so-called 'radical' readings of the Renaissance, Burt is undoubtedly keen to present his research as progressive and, indeed, more enlightened than previous work on censorship. Yet since this progressivism is founded on the concept of the undecidability of the 'final horizon', its incessantly shifting boundaries ironically call to mind the forms of enlightenment/censorship operated in Bensalem and, for that matter, by the simultaneously inclusive and prohibitory strategies of *PMLA*. This is in fact consistent with Burt's contention that censorship and criticism cannot be 'juxtaposed in a stable opposition'.

PART 3

Economies and exchanges

CHAPTER 5

Bringing criticism to account: economy, exchange and cultural theory

In this chapter I want to instance disorientation and leverage in the university by exploring the problematic doubleness of economics as indeterminately both inside and outside contemporary cultural theory. Here, I shall argue that the interdisciplinary approach of cultural analysis has a certain amount of difficulty positioning economics as either simply an outside – an object of critical study or a prior discipline – or an inside – in the form of the very structure of a system of exchange that interdisciplinarity would appear to institute or name. In a similar vein, patterns of consumption within contemporary writing on 'culture' can be understood as the categorised items of an authoritative and knowledgeable critical representation, lending an empirical tone – by way of a certain critical distance – to semiotic and cultural analysis; but they can also be taken to structure academic desire itself which needs to consume in order to know. This disorientation between outside and inside I will link to Derrida's discussion of the gift as that which – in Mauss's *The Gift* – enables a movement from 'cold economic rationality' to 'symbolicity' or '*total social fact*', thereby founding contemporary cultural discourse and, more generally, interdisciplinary work in the humanities and human sciences. In this context, the orientation and leverage within the university apparently offered by the development of cultural studies and by certain forms of interdisciplinarity comes at the cost of an irresolvable disorientation between the object and the activity of criticism, such that cultural analysis continually and undecidably affirms/negates its 'other', endlessly doing itself violence, endlessly antagonising itself.

The chapter comprises four sections. The first raises the question of the interdisciplinary nature of cultural analysis, particularly in relation to the complex interchange between the economy of such criticism – the exchange undertaken between the formation and development of its academic field and the recognition and appropriation of other forms and spaces of knowledge – and the location and deployment of the field of economics itself within this intellectual and discursive economy. In order to account for the problematic yet productive interaction between cultural criticism's own economy and the field of economics, the second section turns to the question of gift-exchange that has so interested theorists this century working across the various disciplines of anthropology, sociology, economics, semiotics and philosophy. It is here I argue that the question of the gift, as formulated by Derrida in particular, raises important questions of the economy and exchange of academic discourse generally. More specifically, in examining Derrida's reading of Mauss, I suggest that cultural criticism is itself organised around the concept of the gift as a prime mover in the shift from cruder forms of economic determinism to the formation and analysis of the 'symbolicity' of the economic that underpins a discourse of culture. While section two tracks the philosophical dimensions and exegesis of Derrida's problem of the gift, the third section focuses more specifically on the implications for cultural criticism of the close relationship between the concept of the gift and that of culture itself arising from Derrida's discussion. The final section traces a line of reflection between the concerns found in Derrida's recent work on the gift and some of the themes emerging earlier in 'Violence and metaphysics', in order to pose the question of critical responsibility in the context of the problematic relationship between the economy of cultural discourse and analysis and the concept and field of culture as constituted by the 'symbolicity' of the economic.

This chapter does not, therefore, simply disparage interdisciplinarian cultural criticism as hopelessly disoriented, but affirms the horizon of the interdisciplinary as a limit of coherence requiring maxmimal responsibility from today's academics. This recognition of the risks and demands of interdisciplinarity links this to the following chapter, where I argue that deconstruction's survival at the limit of coherence of impossibly constituted debates concerning theory's 'life' or 'death' holds the promise for theory's future and in fact persistently raises the issue of responsibility in the vicinity of a modern interdisciplinary university whose exchanges actually exceed final determination or controlled regulation (as the debate 'for' and 'against' deconstruction or theory shows). If, as we saw in the last chapter, the (re)positioning of academic boundaries, especially shifting and thus incessant ones, remains vital in the crossing or journey towards enlightenment, so that the instability of institutional limits may be longstanding and in a certain way functional or productive rather than indicative of a new crisis or sudden moment of breakdown, then nevertheless the limit of coherence of interdisciplinary cultural theory and study suggests a fundamentally disorienting situation which needs to be understood and grasped as both an intractable problem and an opportunity in absolute terms.

Interdisciplinary confusion and the place of the market

As Julie Thompson Klein has noted, interdisciplinarity is 'a concept of wide appeal' but 'also one of wide confusion'.[1] This is no doubt partly because interdisciplinarity has in many cases been attempted at locally identified and often unstable sites of struggle, transformation and development in the field of knowledge, calling for the implementation of myriad forms of theory, methodology and pedagogical practice which themselves would have no claim to universal principle or shared value. Indeed, in challenging notions of rational coherence and orderly activity associated with a discipline, interdisciplinarity – while operating at very particular conjunctions – seems to will such 'wide confusion': this break with discipline itself might be taken to provide a broader definition (if not an *anti*-definition) of interdisciplinarity, or at least an explanation of its almost viral spread from limited to broader contexts in recent times. However, by unproblematically turning 'confusion' into a positive attribute, a veritable life-force unfolding as a sign of the future, a discussion of interdisciplinarity along these lines risks ignoring certain key questions that Klein suggests need to be asked in order to understand the interdisciplinary stakes. Such questions include: 'how did the concept evolve in the twentieth century?'; 'what kinds of activities are associated with it, and why did they emerge?'; 'what is the relationship between disciplinarity and interdisciplinarity?'; 'what happens when interdisciplinary fields begin to assume disciplinary characteristics?'.[2] Taken together, the questions Klein raises indicate that the historicity or temporal dimension of the concept and practice of interdisciplinarity is indispensable in the appreciation of its 'confusions', and that this historicity or temporality is inextricable with that of the concept and practices of a discipline itself.

The intricacies of the emergence and development, in different contexts, of interdisciplinary theory and practice necessitate fuller consideration than is possible here: to this end, Klein's study of the discourse and activity of interdisciplinarity in the late twentieth century provides a most useful account. What I want to do in this chapter is to pursue the question of the relationship between disciplinarity and interdisciplinarity, between the formation of academic fields and identities and the recognition and appropriation of other forms and spaces of knowledge, at the hub of Klein's interrogations of the interdisciplinary project, by taking as an 'example' the positioning of economics within the cross-fertilised space of the modern humanities. This offers a special case, but also a way of addressing some of the issues that primarily concern Klein. The interdisciplinary project – involving, as Klein puts it, 'different types and levels of integrative activity' (p. 11) – may be said to constitute complex processes of exchange between academic fields; or, in Bourdieu's terms, a sophisticated marketplace of specialised knowledges.[3] This immediately raises the question of the 'economic' as inseparable from the concept of interdisciplinarity. For this reason, however, it would seem that economics cannot straightforwardly be assimilated by or appropriated to an interdisciplinary approach, as if interdisciplinarity as a kind of subject were treating economics as its 'object', since the 'economic' provides in advance the terms – metaphorical or otherwise – upon which such an enterprise can be conceived. On the other hand, it seems equally possible to say that economics cannot stand 'outside' interdisciplinary activity as a vantage point or, as it were, a grand narrative of its operations, since such interdisciplinarity, rather than simply constituting itself as an 'object' of the discipline and discourse of economics, functions as a system of exchanges or an economy which, if it does anything at all, flouts disciplinary boundaries and authorities.

Thus, the 'economic'/economics defies any simple positioning either inside or outside the interdisciplinary enterprise. Economics, as the sign of systems of exchange, almost *names* interdisciplinarity, and yet it exists and can be located only problematically in relation to it. Correspondingly, it has been difficult for 'progressive', interdisciplinarian academics and institutions confidently to assert a decidable relationship to the 'economic' both at the conceptual level and in practical terms. In much recent criticism, economics has either been mapped familiarly as essential background to literary and cultural production, which risks leaving intact the text–context/infrastructure–superstructure divisions observed within traditional forms of socioeconomic historicism (as often occurs in cultural materialism, particularly in regard to studies of the early modern period); or otherwise, if considered at all, it has been represented primarily at the symbolic or semiological level as just another feature of the wider social 'text', its specificity denied (as happens in much new historicist criticism). Whether by means of exclusion, marginalisation or contextualisation (economics as an 'outside'), or assimilation and containment (economics as an 'inside'), we find criticism here either *disengaging* differences, redrawing firm borderlines between disciplinary fields, or dissolving and repudiating differences altogether, so that such treatments of economics preserve precisely the kinds of boundaries, spaces and contours of recognition and formations of identity within the field of knowledge that the interdisciplinary project is supposed to call into question.

More complexly, these two versions of the 'economic' – economics as a material base, and economics as a structure of representation (or part of one) – can sometimes be seen contradictorily to interact and overlap within contemporary critical practice. Cultural theory and analysis in regard to Renaissance studies again offers a useful example here. 'Nothing has so consistently underwritten recent efforts to historicize the study of Renaissance drama,' Christopher Pye has written, 'as a perceived connection between economic commodification and representation'.[4] A number of critics have been concerned to theorise cultural production and crisis in the early modern period in terms of seemingly unbounded processes of commodification producing symbolic confusions undermining identity at the level both of the social and the subject. Pye notes in particular Jean-Christophe Agnew's *Worlds Apart* which emphasises the extent to which 'the newly liquid market' and the 'protean character of the theatre' in sixteenth- and seventeenth-century England can be seen as mutually implicated in prompting what Agnew terms 'a crisis of representation' bearing on identity as such.[5] Pye takes as an example of this perceived correspondence between problems of economy and representation the 'not-so-obscurely intertwined proliferation of anti-theatrical and anti-usury tracts during the era, each declaring the limitless shame of a cultural transformation that threatened to reduce all to a groundless play of terms' (p. 502). 'Yet it is precisely the sweeping and fundamental nature of such a transformation,' he suggests, 'that raises methodological qualms'. The sense of 'apprehension' felt by writers of these kinds of tracts indicates, so Pye believes, a degree of externality or alienation in relation to 'the threatened transformation' which itself often appears to harbour 'a groundless play of terms', placing under erasure both its own origins or empirical identity and, by necessary extension, the grounding of the subject and of speech. And, of course, this contradiction or impossibility would also problematise the relationship between the totalising force of much new historicist criticism, which theorises difference, fragmentation and marginalia in terms of generalising concepts and representational strategies of 'arbitrary connectness' and 'circulation' (suggesting the 'liquidity' of the entire social field), and the grounding of this critical discourse which itself seems drawn to such groundless play. In particular, the 'empirical aura' that, according to Pye, clings to the 'economic language' (p. 503) serving to legitimise new historicist cultural poetics is itself undermined by the problem of ungrounded representation which, those poetics argue, is inextricable with the operations and effects of economy in the early modern period.

Conceptual difficulties in deciding the place of economics within contemporary critical practice, giving rise to methodological problems and contradictions of the kind indicated above, have been matched by confusions of a much more practical and immediate nature. More than ever before, criticism has become aware of the existence and the needs, limitations and possibilities of the market. The expansion in higher education since the 1960s has increased numbers of postgraduate students and researchers, creating an atmosphere of aggressive competition, while the reward system brought to bear on professional academics has placed a strong emphasis on the speedy production of books and articles. Awareness of the market has only been heightened by its recent contraction: the number of new academic posts continues to fall due to government funding cuts and the end of a relative 'boom' caused by the creation of new universities in the early 1990s; while publishing houses become evermore cautious and unreceptive to new researchers and projects perceived not to be viable economically. There is everywhere a pressing, almost fatalistic sense that as academics we all exist within – and can only produce ourselves in relation to – a market. To an important extent, this recognition is played out in, and partly explains, the emphasis on and populist identification with consumption that has been happening in cultural studies for some years now. Of particular relevance here are theorisations of the critical or subversive possibilities of consumption, whereby the consumer is no longer imagined as a passive dupe but an active agent and critic, resisting and transforming the system by participation in it (the bestowal, according to Dick Hebdige, of 'forbidden meanings' upon commodities in youth subcultures,[6] for example, or, more recently, the political effectivity of consumer choice, selective buying and boycott described by Mica Nava[7]) rather than challenging it by straightforward opposition and refusal (which translates, in classic Marxist terms, into the withdrawal of labour). If the consumer can be imagined to be a critic, then similarly it is okay for the critic to be a consumer, to 'buy into' and operate guiltlessly within a market system rather than take the career-threatening step of refusing the dominant competitive logic of higher education today, which would perhaps have been the call to arms twenty years ago.

But this rapproachment with the market has by no means been unproblematic for criticism. Let us return to just one example, operating at the most practical level – but also arguably at one of the most concentrated points – of an interaction between contemporary literary and cultural criticism and the evermore visible existence and concept of economy or 'economics'. This in fact will allow us to recapitulate some of the arguments made in the previous chapter. In a recent editorial column of *PMLA*, the journal of the Modern Language Association of America, Domna C. Stanton, as we have seen, justifies the decision taken by the editorial board not to review articles under consideration by other journals.[8] The adoption of this policy against multiple submissions is presented here as a necessary strategic response to 'market forces' in higher education of the kind I have outlined above, which it is argued have caused a crisis in academic 'writing practices' and 'ethical codes', creating a situation in which frenzied textual activity and the unregulated circulation of countless papers has threatened to devastate the established reading practices of refereed journals. Thus, argues Stanton, the policy against multiple submissions is a positive, modernising step intended to improve the treatment of academic authors by enabling the review process to be expedited, as henceforth there would be fewer submissions to be dealt with by editorial staff and referees at any given time. Far from promoting repressive activity, then, this sort of 'censorship' in fact assists the process of bringing academic writing into the public domain, and as such might be thought of as *productive*. Within this formulation of the present, the academy as a liberal 'protected zone'[9] is reconceptualised as a *protective* one, and the market located in a certain way as an 'outside', an intrusive, external menace that pre-exists the response made to it by *PMLA*. However, the market as an 'outside' is also in an important sense an 'inside'. Although Stanton tries implicitly to externalise the writers who are causing so much chaos by drawing a distinction between, on the one hand, 'advisory committees' or 'editorial boards' made up of established, tenured academics (primarily imagined as *readers*) and, on the other, industrious authors, 'especially academics who are beginning their careers' (primarily imagined as *producers*), it cannot be ignored that these writers are also constituents of the MLA, since submissions by members only are given consideration. (They are also, confusingly, *readers*, since membership entails subscription to *PMLA*.) By muddling its terms, therefore, the debate itself points to the externalisation of an internal menace: the market as the name for the 'otherness' existing nonetheless at the origins of the academy's own identity. Indeed, in a way that contradicts the externalisation of 'market forces' found elsewhere in her column, Stanton at one point passes off the policy against multiple submissions as the outcome of an internal and largely self-reflexive economy of resources and production, managing a kind of self-regulation or *self*-censorship. This sense of internality, of a joint enterprise and of mutually beneficial limitation, enables Stanton to imagine a reconnection with the membership. They are henceforth reassuringly included once more in *PMLA* business (their annual dues no doubt borne in mind) rather than positioned as a prohibited outsider. But now market conditions are very differently envisaged. They exist institutionally, in Bourdieu's terms, as 'a *compromise* between the *expressive interest* and a *censorship* constituted by the very structure of the field',[10] placing *intrinsic* and, indeed, enabling constraints upon the very process of discursive production. In terms of the multiple submissions debate, which points up numerous anxieties within the culture of academic institutions today, the market therefore remains undecidable, oscillating between its location as 'outside', where it is configured as a material basis prior to superstructural or ideological forms like (academic) culture, language or criticism, and its location as an 'inside', where it is configured as the very structuration of representation which actually determines what can be produced or consumed (i.e. written or read). The market becomes undecidable as a negative or positive thing, made up simultaneously of difference and sameness, and thought of both in terms of a distant horizon and a preconditional field.

   In fact, this double and contradictory positioning of the market can be traced throughout the development of cultural studies itself. While there is not sufficient space here to provide a thoroughgoing account of this development, one can see that, for example, from Adorno and Horkheimer's 'The culture industry'[11] – which in its meticulously detailed invective against mass culture shows that to criticise popular forms one must first know and consume them – to more recent optimistic and populist work – which not only identifies *with* and connects to the popular, but also relentlessly identifies it *as* an object of study ripe for the contemplative gaze of the academic spectator – it is not simply the case that the market is, for cultural criticism, *either* a negative *or* a positive, *either* an 'outside' *or* an 'inside', an external material base or an inclusive structure of representation. Rather, it is in its doubleness as both inside/outside that the market structures the discursive processes – the very production – of cultural criticism. For instance, in Nava's chapter 'Consumerism reconsidered: buying and power' (operating within the by-now familiar contours of cultural studies), the continual naming and listing of popular groups and forms such as 'ordinary people', 'women shoppers', 'the young', 'black hairstyles', 'video games', 'sound systems and computers' reproduces the identificatory and distancing effects traditionally associated with the formation of academic knowledge, as much as it produces an image of the popular which provides 'something to identify with', 'something which is much more exciting and fashionable' for the 'postmodern' academic as well as the postwar populace.[12] Patterns of consumption can here be identified as the categorised objects of authoritative representation, now at one remove from the academic discourse that speaks of them through the unavoidable reinscription of critical distance; but they can also be taken to structure academic desire itself which must consume if it is to know. Again, consumption – as an analogue of the market or the 'economic' – is undecidably and antagonistically both inside and outside, invested with an empirical aura through which concepts of culture are legitimated, while also indicating the internal psychic or discursive conditions and possibilities of criticism prior to its discovery and articulation of the 'object'.

It will be recalled that this doubleness is in fact repeated and reproduced in Greenblatt's new historicist work, which has contributed another dimension to cultural theory and analysis by drawing together various heterogeneous strands from anthropology, semiotics, New Criticism, Marxism and poststructuralism in the development of what Greenblatt has termed 'cultural poetics'. In 'Towards a poetics of culture', written to offer some kind of account of new historicist aims and objectives in the field of cultural inquiry, Greenblatt remarks that 'the oscillation between totalisation and difference, uniformity and ... diversity ... unitary truth and a proliferation of distinct entities' found in the differing views of late capitalism held by Lyotard and Jameson 'depends less upon poststructuralist theory' than upon the 'poetics' – the 'everyday' cultural forms – of contemporary American politics and society.[13] For Greenblatt, the economy of culture is too complex, too multidimensional and, finally, too unknowable to be appropriated straightforwardly as the 'content' of the economy of academic discourse. As I argued in Chapter 2, the impetus here seems to be to short-circuit the idea that the agency of culture and cultural exchange can somehow be reduced to postmodern language games or theoretical paradigms. However, such unstable slippage between 'distinct entities' or 'discontinuous discourses' on the one hand and 'totalisation' or 'monologic unification' on the other can be found, in the introductory chapter of *Shakespearean Negotiations* for example, to structure in similarly inconsistent ways Greenblatt's own representational strategies and methodological manoeuvrings. Here, a view of Shakespeare's plays as the product of a 'sublime confrontation' between 'a total artist and a totalising society' – between the masterful poet and a near Tillyardian social totality in which all parts express the whole via seamless inclusion and organic interplay – is discarded in favour of a more deconstructive picture of the writer as 'constructed out of conflicting and ill-sorted motives', and a vaguely Marxist view that 'Elizabethan and Jacobean images of hidden unity seemed like anxious rhetorical attempts to conceal cracks, conflict and disarray'.[14] This move from totalisation to discontinuity is, however, negotiated precisely through a totalising gesture: the now fragmented, decentred Shakespeare nevertheless *wholly* expresses and reflects the portrayal of Renaissance culture and society as multiform and contradictory, giving renewed impetus to new historicism's methodological principle of 'arbitary connectedness', which, as Walter Cohen has put it, allows difference to be analysed within 'generalising inferences'.[15] Unbound by any traditional historical sense or paradigm, the formalism of new historicism's seemingly limitless linkages between cultural minutiae enables an inclusive structure to enter in by the back door of contemporary criticism, rubbing against the grain of its anecdotal accounts of what is supposedly marginal, partial, erratic, or fragmented. From this perspective, the particular formation of the market as characterised by an 'oscillation between totalisation and difference' that Greenblatt seeks to externalise in relation to 'theory' actually comes to describe, from the outset, the ambivalent and confused processes of formation, the unresolved exchange between sameness and difference, found in new historicist methodology itself.

We therefore arrive at two analoguous problems. One the one hand, we have the indeterminate location of economics within the interdisciplinary project of the modern humanities, whereby the difficulties and perhaps even embarrassment caused by its awkward and ambiguous status leads either to a stealthy reversion to traditional forms of socioeconomic historicism and scholarship, or to the subsumption and effective silencing of the 'economic' within post-Marxist readings of culture, or to a confused and unsatisfactory mixture of the two. And, on the other, we have the confusion that not only troubles cultural criticism's positioning of itself in relation to the market, but which actually structures (through an unstable fluctuation between inside/outside) a great deal of its thinking, making possible much of what it has had to say. The possibility of some linkage between these two problems – the problem of the economy of interdisciplinary work generally and of cultural criticism specifically – is what I am most concerned to explore here. There would be various ways to do this, the most obvious perhaps being a return to the differing views held by Jameson and Lyotard concerning the workings of the 'economic' and of the market in general, culminating famously in the dispute about (the cultural logic of) the postmodern as a figure of late capitalism (it is also, of course, the figure of late twentieth-century academic discourse). However, this approach may very well involve simply retracing, and ultimately remaining trapped within, the kinds of 'restless oscillations' between sameness and difference, 'uniformity' and 'diversity', 'unitary truth and a proliferation of distinct entities' that Greenblatt identifies as structuring both the 'postmodern' debate and the late capitalist condition: an oscillation which, as we have seen, also characterises and ensnares his own discourse and methodology. To stay within the terms of reference of Greenblatt's essay may therefore involve reproducing, unwittingly, the confusions I'd like to attempt to untangle. I want therefore to explore the economy of criticism by turning instead to the question of the gift that for many years has interested exchange theorists working within and across the disciplinary fields of anthropology, sociology, economics, semiotics and philosophy. In particular, the question of the gift may prove important to the discussion of interdisciplinary work and the status of an account such as is produced by cultural criticism, inasmuch as it has been posed more recently by Derrida so as to raise issues of the economy and exchange of academic discourse itself. Furthermore, it may be seen from Derrida's discussion that the concept of the gift is of great importance in understanding the problems of cultural criticism specifically, since the gift emerges here as a prime mover in the shift from cold economism to the formation and analysis of the 'symbolicity' of the economic that underpins the totalising discourse of 'culture'.

Before turning to Derrida's work on the question of the gift, however, it may be helpful to sketch very briefly some of the main lines of development of theories of gift-exchange this century, in order more properly to situate some of the themes arising out of Derrida's exploration of the problem. As we will see, Marcel Mauss's groundbreaking inquiry into the question of the gift within the field of anthropology attempted to show that exchange rituals in archaic societies, rather than operating simply at the level of individual activity, established well-organised, collective relations within a generalised economy.[16] In contrast, Georges Bataille's reading of Mauss's *The Gift*, locatable in a quite different, radical tradition of social-scientific thought, calls into question the more or less stable and functional patterns of bestowal and reciprocity within this generalised economy, emphasising and celebrating instead the symbolic centrality of expenditure without reserve, of destructive wastage, manifested in the potlatch.[17] Later theorists such as Jean Baudrillard and indeed Derrida himself have drawn attention to the fact that the elaborate and extravagant squandering of wealth characterising the potlatch nevertheless produces a significant return in the form of universal respect, approbation and social status, ruling out the possibility of an entirely one-sided and therefore wholly expended gift. However, Bataille's rethinking of the significance of the gift marks an important theoretical shift in relation to Mauss, inasmuch as Bataille locates excessive usage to the point of violence and destruction – manifested in the sacralised events of exorbitance found in the potlatch – as the central principle upon which premodern forms of social organisation and economy are predicated, suggesting an important idea of the practical realisation and fulfilment of use-value only in and by means of its expense. For Baudrillard, working partly on the basis of an engagement with Bataille's work, the productivist and utilitarian imperatives of modern capitalism have sought to exclude archaic, symbolic rituals of loss of the kind manifested in the potlatch, but have nevertheless produced new forms of excess through the spiralling velocity of sign-value within the semiotic and simulational orders extending from the early modern period to the present.[18] Thus the notions of excess, destruction and loss, as they relate to gift-exchange, are complicated by Baudrillard in his analysis of the formations of contemporary capitalism, since excess cannot be seen as existing in a straightforward conceptual or historical opposition to utility. Rather, the generalised exchange of sign-values in modern capitalist society has brought about a set of circumstances (not so much a mode, as a code) in which the operations of pure use-value or utility – existing as the very ideal of modernity – become impossible: 'Ours is a society founded on proliferation, on growth which continues even though it cannot be measured against any clear goals ... The upshot is gross systemic congestion and malfunction caused by ... an excess of functional imperatives, by a sort of saturation'.[19] Sign-value as a principle of exchange within modernity produces itself according to an excess which destabilises any utile division of semiotic or discursive space, giving itself in such a way that, paradoxically, its own energies become malfunctional as an expression of the system's functions. Baudrillard's work, in particular on gift-exchange, therefore establishes an interesting context in which Derrida's contribution to the question of the gift can be read since, in the latter, the gift (as an expression of an academic discourse that in turn gives itself in the form of an account) generates uncontainable kinds of friction and supplementary disturbance, comparable I will argue to the violence which concerns Derrida's 'Violence and metaphysics' (1978), that can be located as a condition of otherwise ostensibly productive patterns of exchange within the discursive process.

Rendering an account

Before coming to the implications that Derrida's contemplation of the question of gift has for the kinds of problems in cultural theory I have outlined so far, it is important to begin by looking at how (and from where) this discussion proceeds on philosophical terms. In two essays forming part of *Given Time* (1992), 'The time of the king' and 'The madness of economic reason', Derrida turns his attention to Mauss's aforementioned anthropological study of the economic function of the gift within primitive human societies. Mauss argues that here the gift functions to establish complex systems and networks of exchange, reciprocity, debt, obligation, status and deferment, not so much in place of money which might otherwise be thought properly to belong to developed societies, but as a kind of money itself. While Derrida acknowledges the concept of the gift as 'related to economy', he nevertheless asks 'is not the gift, if there is any, also that which interrupts economy? That which, in suspending economic calculation, no longer gives rise to exchange?'.[20] In other words, for the gift truly to exist or to be given, reciprocity, obligation, debt – as particular formations of the general principle of exchange – must be absolutely dispensed with or forgotten. In Mauss's analysis, however, these forms of exchange represent the indispensable condition and meaning of the gift, constituting its very purpose. To this extent, Derrida suggests that Mauss's *The Gift*, in dealing with 'economy, exchange, contract', 'speaks of everything but the gift' (p. 24). Indeed, Derrida goes so far as to propose that even the recognition of a gift as gift implicitly binds the donee into a logic of exchange (perhaps Mauss is himself bound into this logic also, as the 'knowing' recipient of a kind of gift itself taking the form of recognition, discovery and anthropological knowledge of archaic societies). The gift once identified as gift inevitably bears 'the mark of a duty, a debt owed, of the duty not-to ... even not to give back', although of course the acknowledgement of a gift as gift cannot avoid giving something back, in the form of the acknowledgement itself (this need not even take the form of gratitude since, as Derrida points out, a gift can amount to 'hurting, to doing harm' because it 'puts the other in debt'). Recognition of the gift 'gives back, in the place ... of the thing itself, a symbolic equivalent' (pp. 12–13) – just as Mauss gives a symbolic (and semantic) equivalent, his book *The Gift*, in recognition of the gift which, ostensibly, it is about, but which according to Derrida it also effectively annuls through the particular kind of exchange (between the gift and *The Gift*) taking place.

The philosophical problem of the gift as it is crystallised by Derrida is therefore this: the conditions of possibility of the gift, which he formulates in terms of 'someone *intends-to-give* something to someone' (p. 10), constitute simultaneously the conditions of its impossibility. The formula given by Derrida (we will come back to the problem of this 'given', of the academic's bequest, as one we have already begun to track in regard to Mauss's 'knowing' textual exchange with the gift) supposes, as Derrida recognises (again, for similar reasons, this 'recognition' may also interest us), a number of identifications which annihilate the gift: not only the acknowledgement of 'something' given, which destroys it; but also the formation of the 'constituted subject' of both donor and donee, who thereby enter into a logic of reciprocation or contract; and in particular the identification of 'someone' (an individual or an anthropomorphised group) that gives, and through 'the gesture of the gift' has its 'own identity recognized so that that identity comes back to it, so it can reappropriate its identity: as its property' (pp. 10–11). Thus, the gift as given within this formula inevitably leads, by way of patterns of real and symbolic investment and return in which the identity of the possessive individual is (re)appropriated, to property rights and relations which ruin it *as* gift. The cycle of circulation and of *returning* self-evidently opposes its very idea. Here, the concept of 'return' that irrevocably damages the gift evokes not only an idea of profit but also introduces a dimension of time. For the gift to be possible, this 'ritual circle of the debt' (p. 23) incurred by giving must therefore undergo what Derrida terms 'effraction' or interruption, in a time which, paradoxically and impossibly we might think, constitutes itself as an instant. This – perhaps unattainable – spontaneity is nevertheless vital because the gift, if it is to exist at all, cannot exist in a time characterised by deferral, by temporal lag or delay, by temporality itself as an interplay between presence/absence, through which patterns, cycles, circles of investment, accumulation, deferment, debt and return necessarily return (both Derrida and Lyotard in *The Differend* suggest that (exchange-)value is nothing more than stored up time):[21] the gift must literally be nothing other than present.

The intention-to-give involves, however, a recognition – 'someone *intends-to-give* something to someone' – which necessitates or which takes a time. To this extent, as Derrida is well aware, the philosophical contemplation, recognition of and return to the problem of the gift – even the knowing *giving* of a formula that suggests the gift's possibility/impossibility – leads us not away from methodological problems (those associated with Mauss, for example) but brings us back to the heart of them. Indeed, the paradox of the gift as acknowledged by Derrida threatens to trap critical discourse in a circle or cycle whereby the problem is compounded in the very process of unravelling it. As Derrida himself notes, the very context of his paper 'The time of the king' is characterised by 'an unsigned but effective contract between us [addresser:addressee/donor:donee: the speaker and his audience, but now also the writer and the reader], indispensable to what is happening here, namely that you accord, lend or give some attention and some meaning to what I myself am doing by giving, for example, a lecture' (p. 11). Even if dissatisfaction is expressed on receipt of the gift Derrida gives the donee (audience/reader), 'even if in a little while we were to argue or disagree about everything', nevertheless sufficent 'good faith' is shown or enough respect and 'credit' paid the event that it fulfils the terms of a contract, a calculated exchange. Yet this return to the logic of contract, and to the 'ritual circle of debt', generosity and gratitude that typifies and surrounds conventions of public speaking in the academic setting, annuls any gift Derrida might hope to give, subsuming the much-regarded and wished-for 'object' of analysis under the dense fabric of intellectual exchanges, investments and approbations which intrinsically oppose it.

It is this very problem that Derrida struggles with towards the end of his lecture. Here, he insists, 'If one must *render an account* (to science, to reason, to philosophy, to the economy of meaning) of the circle effects in which a gift gets annulled, this account-rendering requires that one take into account that which, while not simply belonging to the circle, engages it and sets it off in motion' (p. 31): that is, the gift itself, which exists both within the economic circle, contracted almost inevitably 'into a circular contract' or logic of exchange, but which crucially also appears as the 'first mover of the circle', the prior or suppositional term of the 'someone *intends-to-give* something to someone' upon which the circle or cycle, the whole economy, spins. It would seem that what Derrida is saying here is that the paradoxical and unresolvable conditions of possibility/impossibility of the gift produce themselves as a kind of incalculable madness, generating an irrational excess in excess of the circle's economy, this 'otherness' harbouring the potential perhaps for a way out of the circular trap in which criticism seems to be caught in regard to the problem of the gift. And yet to *render an account* to someone or something (reason, philosophy, the economy of meaning) of this excess would surely entail a return to the logic of contract and calculation which this excess exceeds but also relentlessly 'sets off [in] motion'? Indeed, Derrida in the same passage describes this 'account-rendering' in terms of 'the contract between us, for this cycle of lectures', recognising once more the ironic impossibility underlying the conditions of possibility of his lectures on the gift.

Subsequently, Derrida wrestles with the need to render an account, if only of the possibility of a simulacrum of the gift, which in turn entails for him a question of desire: what impels Derrida toward this account-rendering? Why would he wish to commit himself, to obligate himself, to the impossible task of rendering an account of the gift? The question is in one respect arrived at naturally, since as we have seen the issue under discussion provides a model, a paradigm or analogue for the difficulty of academic discourse and practice itself: giving an account. Hence, mirroring the problem of the impossible possibility of the gift, Derrida contemplates the paradoxical calling which urges him 'to answer ... for a gift that calls one beyond all responsibility' (p. 31). To pursue the difficult question of the gift, even of the excess and irresponsibility of the gift, nevertheless again compels Derrida to move *responsibly* within the circles of credit, debt, deferment, respect, generosity and gratitude/reward that constitute the economy of academic discourse and community: this returns him and us to the impossibility of simply *giving* an account, of course. Although we now seem to have reached a stage in the argument or analysis when it becomes impossible to do anything other than repeat the problem, indeed to write repetitiously of it, nevertheless this brings us near a moment in the discussion at which it becomes possible to use Derrida's contemplation of the gift to account for and evaluate cultural criticism's unstable economy of circulation between inside and outside, subject and object, same and different, the issue with which we began.

Culture and the gift

One way of putting Derrida's problem of the gift, if it does not ensnare us in yet more circularity, is that the gift (such as any gift Derrida might wish to give the academic community in the – impossible – form of an account) cannot travel, cannot go anywhere, i.e. *from* self *to* other. Even if it remained unacknowledged in explicit ways as gift, untouched by the 'circle of debt' we have recognised as the academy's culture, the given account in travelling from one place to another, from A to B, from someone to someone else, would still suppose and implicitly constitute the subject both of donor and donee, inscribing reciprocity, the exchange of identities, within a time or temporality (the lag between donor and donee created by the gesture of the gift). Thus, the gift has nowhere to go but itself, and furthermore to itself as non-gift since it cannot be given, so to itself as non-self. Indeed, the non-self-identicality of the gift, discovered at the moment it returns to itself paradoxically having gone nowhere, implies a difference or a splitting (which comes only from itself, the gift having gone nowhere) which further disrupts and denies the present (presence) of the gift, the gift as present.

The non-self-identicality of the gift, the gift as non-self or non-present at its origins or in its essence, may be precisely what generates the calling for the gift to be given, to consummate itself or find its meaning through a journey or a process of exchange ('someone *intends-to-give* something to someone') in which nevertheless its existence is annulled: an impossible journey, one it must embark upon though which it can never travel; one from which it returns in ruins though ruination was what made it venture forth. This return, then, is found at the very origins of the gift, annihilating it from the outset and yet compelling it once more to set out. The madness of this simultaneity of gift and exchange is remarked upon along similar lines by Derrida in 'The madness of economic reason' inasmuch as here too the gift is presented not simply as the unwitting object of an insidious cycle of exchanges that surrounds and envelops it, as if the struggle waged between the gift and exchange were thinkable merely in terms of the – albeit unequally balanced – clash of opposites. Rather, the simultaneity of gift and exchange emerges in a certain way as a condition of the gift itself, of its own impossibility or madness. 'The contradiction between gift and exchange,' says Derrida, 'leads to madness in the case both where the gift must remain foreign to circular exchange as well as where it is pulled into that exchange, unless it is the gift itself that does the pulling' (p. 39). This suggestion that the gift itself does the pulling, that it may be the agent of its own madness, of its own confusions, emerges within a sentence construction which itself underscores this confusion, this non-self-identicality of the gift: for here it is both foreign and familiar to exchange, simultaneously made possible and impossible in either case, existing and not-existing undecidably as both object and mover in relation to the economic cycle. This non-self-identicality forces the gift to go outside itself – to pull itself outside by 'force' Derrida tells us – to find completion, although of course the outside it travels to emerges as a projection of its own needs, of the difference or doubleness that constitutes its own impossible identity or interiority. As Derrida puts it, 'the requirement of the circulatory *differance is inscribed within the thing itself* that is given or exchanged' (p. 40). The gift's attempt to attain unity, tranquility, transcendence (to become given and a given, to reach an end and find a beginning) is undermined from the outset by those violently restless and impossible fluctuations between sameness and difference that force this journey.

If, as Derrida suggests, the rendering of an account always, at some level, involves entry into the self-rewarding cycles of generosity, gratitude, paying of credit and acknowledgement of debt that surround academic discourse and community, and which thereby preclude 'something' being given by 'someone' to 'someone else', preventing the account actually crossing from A to B, then at the same time his discussion of the problem of the gift develops the idea that, by force of its own contradictions or non-identity, the account as gift nevertheless needs or always desires to make the very journey which only compounds its confusions: to cross always in the form of a non-crossing, to arrive at a place which is only ever a projection of itself as non-self, that is to produce itself only and inseparably by sustaining its own indeterminacy, perplexity and disarray. It is precisely these kinds of confusions, of course, that we tracked in the first part of this essay in relation to various sorts of academic account. Furthermore, such confusions (between inside and outside, subject and object, self and other) can be specifically located in an academic discourse founded on a discussion of the relationship between gift and exchange, since – as we have seen in several examples from Derrida – this 'discursive gesture is from the outset an example of that about which it claims to be speaking' (p. 62). And it is the discussion of the relationship between gift and exchange which, as Derrida suggests in his study of Mauss, instigates a seismic shift from traditional forms of economism, through anthropology, sociology, structuralism and linguistics, to contemporary cultural criticism and interdisciplinary work in the humanities generally. For Derrida, Mauss's stubborn insistence on the word and category of the gift characterises the critical moment at which social theory seeks boldly to transcend 'cold economic rationality' by describing the 'symbolicity' of this rationality (the gift as the 'symbolic' form of economic and social exchange and value in primitive societies), thus enabling 'an account of religious, cultural, ideological, discursive, esthetic, literary, poetic phenomena' under the rubric of the 'economic' (p. 42). Put another way, this recourse to the question of the gift within economic thought or reason enables academic discourse to speak of *total social fact* – or culture – by formulating, conceptualising, organising the 'economic' within the problem of the gift. Indeed, as Derrida tells us, (Mauss's) recognition of the gift itself 'gives back, in the place ... of the thing itself, a symbolic equivalent' (pp. 12–13), thus enabling a move from cruder economic determinism to 'symbolicity', and hence – as we have seen in the last twenty or thirty years – to cultural theory and analysis. From this perspective, it is possible to see the question of the gift as originary in relation to contemporary cultural criticism itself, setting off as 'first mover' its seemingly limitless interdisciplinary exchanges regulated by way of the totalising term: culture. Moreover, if we follow unswervingly Derrida's line of thought here, cultural criticism, when speaking of the economic in ways which go beyond cold economism, must necessarily be speaking of the gift, since it is the category and concept of the gift that has allowed cultural criticism to manoeuvre itself into this position, to open its discursive formation of the economic as the discursivity of the economic, which we have located for example in the doubleness of cultural studies' or new historicism's relation to exchange, consumption and the market. For cultural criticism, the gift is always inseparable from the economic since without it the economic could not be spoken of or about in its own terms of 'culture'.

To summarise, then: cultural criticism can be thought of as the name for a particular formation or line of academic discourse founded on the category of gift, which in seeking to render an account of economics or the economic within its own interdisciplinary field will therefore be required – even if this is unacknowledged – to work within the context of, to have recourse to, and thereby implicitly *to give an account of* the gift. And, of course, Derrida has drawn our attention to the impossible conditions of such a process, although again we need to note that this impossibility lies at the origins of cultural criticism's possibility, since to say anything at all about the economic, and by extension about anything at all since cultural criticism's object is '*total social fact*' located within the 'symbolicity' of the economic, it must speak of the gift. Interdisciplinary criticism in the humanities gives itself, and gives an account of itself, only by means of theoretical and methodological recourse to an idea of culture which operates at the juncture between symbolism and materialism, that is where economics functions on the symbolic level. This juncture, then, is one at which, through tracking a complicated philosophical exegesis of a problem, we can see the concept of culture and the concept of the gift having become inseparably fused and confused. And this doubling of culture and the gift in the very *formation* of cultural criticism suggests a reason for the inadequately differentiated interplay between inside and outside, subject and object, external materiality and representational interiority, that arises (as a precondition) at the moment cultural criticism *gives* an account of culture.

Culture and responsibility

In the last part of this chapter I want to come back to the issue of critical responsibility that arises, however briefly, at the moment Derrida finds himself struggling under the apparently self-inflicted burden of a need to account for the tantalisingly unattainable object of his interest, the 'other' at the heart of his discourse which, it seems, is ceaselessly displaced and lost in the very process of naming, identifying, speaking of it. I want to turn to another, much earlier essay by Derrida, perhaps his best known, to explore the way in which the concept of critical responsibility is confronted and addressed in the face of the many difficulties and dilemmas associated with academic discourse; difficulties and dilemmas of the kind described in the essays on the gift we have looked at so far. This crucial emphasis on responsibility is often overlooked in crude readings of Derrida which locate his work at the origins of various kinds of irresponsible pessimism and frivolous intellectual elitism which have been seen by conservatives (in universities, in the media and elsewhere) to undermine both the critical authority of the academy (and, by extension, other traditional social institutions) and more generally the cultural fabric of post-1960s society. By introducing a concept of critical responsibility into a discussion of the problems of cultural criticism arising out of Derrida's work, it becomes possible to counter this line of critique, and to show how, for Derrida, the problems that arise in any analytical discourse (such as cultural criticism itself offers, for example) demand rigorously thought-out – and, one might say, more realistic – critical attitudes, strategies and techniques rather than any abandonment of a responsible critical stance.

The themes that arise in the essays we have concentrated on – in particular the non-self-identical doubleness of same and other, subject and object, that impels the gift's (and therefore cultural criticism's) impossible journey between the two – do in any case emerge classically in Derrida's earlier work, where critical responsibility in light of such problems is a key question. In 'Violence and metaphysics' his reading of the philosophy of Levinas turns upon similar issues. In this essay Derrida pursues the problem of otherness identified in Levinas's claim: '"If the other could be possessed, seized, and known, it would not be other"'.[22] The unattainability, by definition, of otherness within (academic) discourse and knowledge both sparks and frustrates the language and concept of the other, to the extent that the *phenomenon* of the other cannot encounter the other without friction and violence (just as cultural theory cannot encounter the gift as its founding principle without confusion and conflict). And since the other *as* other cannot truly be included or spoken of within a discourse of the other, the friction or violence generated by any given discourse produces only a kind of violence against itself, just as the gift-account in having nowhere to go but itself as non-given and therefore non-self suffers the kinds of self-inflicted damage, perplexity and disarray uncovered in Derrida's work. Thus Derrida remarks, 'Discourse, therefore, if it is originally violent, can only *do itself violence*, can only negate itself in order to affirm itself' (p. 130). However, this violence against itself is of course necessary for discourse to produce itself, to sustain itself, to be and to speak. Such oddly productive violence characterises the antagonistic simultaneity of recognition and neutralisation of the other within discourse, a simultaneity of the kind we have located in a variety of forms of cultural theory, which itself indicates the violent oscillation between the affirmation and negation of the egoity of discourse itself, since the other (in discourse) is really only projected (through a 'strange symmetry whose trace appears nowhere in Levinas's descriptions') as alter-ego: 'the other is absolutely other only if he is an ego, that is, in a certain way, if he is the same as I' (pp. 127–8).

The violence of a discourse of the other, that is of discourse *itself* which must always give itself to something, someone, or some other (as a gift that cannot be given except to itself, or even to itself), obviously cannot be ignored or repressed without compounding the very same kinds of discord and turbulence that set the problem in motion. Even if we might imagine from a reading of Levinas that violence could be abolished by recognising and respecting the irreducible alterity of the other, and thus its egoity, hence 'suspending the difference (conjunction or opposition) between the same and the other', nevertheless such 'eschatology which animates Levinas's discourse would have to have had kept its promise already, even to the extent of no longer being able to occur within discourse as eschato*logy*' (p. 130). The possibility of an end to violence can only be stated through discourse, that is through violence (just as respect for the other – ethics – entails a phenomenology of otherness which necessarily leads straight back to the heart of the problem (p. 121)). To 'overlook the irreducibility of this last violence', the irrevocable conflicts of the discursive formation in which same and other are produced frictionally as non-self-identical doubles, is to revert to a kind of complacent 'dogmatism' in philosophy (p. 130) in which,

Derrida tells us, the question of critical responsibility is not posed – as he himself poses it in 'Violence and metaphysics'.

By pursuing such problems in Derrida's earlier work, a pursuit which in fact exposes a line of reflection between questions of metaphysics and discourse found there and later concerns with economy and culture, it is possible to see that the confusions between same and other that structure, and that contradictorily affirm/negate, interdisciplinarian cultural criticism – particularly in relation to an economic discourse founded on the concept of the gift – require a careful response from today's critics. If the gift, as the sign of the symbolicity of the economic upon which contemporary cultural criticism is founded, 'calls one beyond all responsibility', then nevertheless the obligation to render an account, to answer for, entails a violence which critical discourse must recognise rather than reject in order to be responsible.[23] To subject culture (the field opened by the concept of the gift) to the economy of criticism is to risk an impossible task, beset by irresolvable antagonisms, but to forego – and leave unacknowledged – the violence of (cultural) discourse doing itself violence is to risk a worse violence still.

Notes

1 Julie Thompson Klein, *Interdisciplinarity: History, Theory, and Practice* (Detroit, MI: Wayne State University Press, 1990), p. 11.

2 *Ibid.*, p. 15.

3 Pierre Bourdieu, 'Censorship and the imposition of form', in his *Language and Symbolic Power* (Oxford: Basil Blackwell, 1991).

4 Christopher Pye, 'The theater, the market, and the subject of history', *English Literary History*, 61 (1994) 501–22, p. 501. All further references will be given in the main body of the text.

5 Jean-Christophe Agnew, *Worlds Apart: The Market and the Theater in Anglo-American Thought, 1550–1750* (Cambridge: Cambridge University Press, 1986), pp. 112–13.

6 Dick Hebdige, *Subculture: The Meaning of Style* (London: Methuen, 1979).

7 Mica Nava, *Changing Cultures: Feminism, Youth and Consumerism* (London: Sage, 1992).

8 Domna C. Stanton, 'Editor's column, on multiple submissions', *PMLA* 109:1 (January 1994), 7–13.

9 I have taken this term from Michael Holquist's contribution to the number in question, entitled 'Corrupt originals: the paradox of censorship', *PMLA*

109:1 (January 1994) 14–25. It arises out of the author's discussion of Kant: 'the function that Kant advocated for the philosophical faculty at Konigsberg [was] to serve as a protected zone in which propositions taught in other faculties as unquestionable truths could be freely interrogated' (p. 23). Interestingly while the editor, Domna C. Stanton, tries, albeit unsuccessfully, to present the issue of protection in terms of an absolutely externalised 'other' – the market – in Holquist's essay the confusions between inside and outside are more apparent in the sense that philosophical faculties, it is suggested, need primarily to protect themselves from *other* faculties *within* the academy.

10 Pierre Bourdieu, 'Censorship and the imposition of form', p. 137.

11 Theodor Adorno and Max Horkheimer, 'The culture industry: enlightenment as mass deception', in their *Dialectic of Enlightenment* (London: Verso, 1979).

12 Mica Nava, *Changing Cultures*, p. 194. For a more detailed account of the problematic formation of cultural studies, see Gary Hall, '"It's a thin line between love and hate": why cultural studies is so "naff"', *Angelaki*, 2:2 (1996) 25–46.

13 Stephen Greenblatt, 'Towards a poetics of culture', in *The New Historicism* ed. H. Aram Veeser (London: Routledge, 1989), p. 8.

14 Stephen Greenblatt, *Shakespearean Negotiations: The Circulation of Social Energy in Renaissance England* (California: California University Press, 1987) pp. 1–4.

15 Walter Cohen, 'Political criticism of Shakespeare', in *Shakespeare Reproduced: The Text in History and Ideology* ed. Jean Howard and Marion O' Connor (London: Methuen, 1987), p. 27.

16 Marcel Mauss, *The Gift: The Form and Reason For Exchange in Archaic Societies* (London: Routledge, 1990).

17 See, for example, Georges Bataille, *Visions of Excess: Selected Writings 1927–1939* (Minneapolis, MN: University of Minnesota Press, 1985); *Literature and Evil* (New York: Marion Boyars, 1985); *The Accursed Share*, Volume 1 (New York: Zone Books, 1991).

18 See, for example, Jean Baudrillard, *For a Critique of the Political Economy of the Sign* (New York: Telos Press, 1981); *Symbolic Exchange and Death*, trans. Iain Hamilton Grant (London: Sage, 1993).

19 Jean Baudrillard, *The Transparency of Evil: Essays on Extreme Phenomena* (London: Routledge, 1993), p. 31.

20 Jacques Derrida, *Given Time: 1. Counterfeit Money*, trans. Peggy Kamuf (Chicago, IL and London: University of Chicago Press, 1992), p. 7. All further references will be given in the main body of the text.

21 Jean-Francois Lyotard, *The Differend: Phrases in Dispute* (Minneapolis, MN: University of Minnesota Press, 1988).

22 Jacques Derrida, 'Violence and metaphysics: an essay on the thought of Emmanuel Levinas', in his *Writing and Difference*, trans. Alan Bass (London: Routledge, 1995), p. 91. All further references will be given in the main body of the text.

23 Robert J. C. Young in 'The dialectics of cultural criticism', *Angelaki*, 2:2 (1996) 9–24, ends a long discussion of Adorno's essay 'Cultural criticism and society' by drawing a similar conclusion with respect to the responsibilities of the contemporary critic in the face of irresolvable antagonisms, speaking of 'the need to utilize the more complex antinomies that deploy in a productive way the paradoxical, impossible position of the cultural critic in society' (p. 23).

CHAPTER 6

Surviving theory, '*as if* I[t] were dead'

> from the beginning of, let's say, the institutionalisation of this word
> in academic circles in the Western world people have been saying ...
> it's waning, it's on the wane. I've heard this for the last twenty-five
> years: it's finished, it is dying. Why do I say dying? It is dead! I tell
> you it's dead! ... I'm totally convinced that deconstruction started
> dying from the very first day.
>
> Jacques Derrida, '*As if* I were dead'[1]

If it were possible to separate the two (as Baudrillard claims, and
Derrida does not) I would be tempted to say that this chapter is
about survival, not death. It is driven on the one hand by a familiar
and not in itself sophisticated wish to formulate a less crude
response to those who, while seeing the value of certain theoretical
insights and institutional changes up to a point, were – as it turns
out – always sceptical of theory's (self-) destructively 'nihilistic',
'irrational' and 'irresponsible' excesses (though currently they seem
to delight in them).[2] Those who now admit to a sense of exhaustion
with theory, something they nevertheless seem to have felt all along,
from the beginning (whenever that was). Those who barely attempt
to conceal their relief that it seems to be going away, dying off, and
scarcely disguise a feeling of pleasure at being able to return, perhaps just a little changed, to more traditional forms of research,
scholarship and discipline. As Derrida suggests, such responses
hardly mark the end of theory's time but are instead perhaps characteristic of it: 'people have been saying ... it's waning ... from the
very first day'. On the other hand, the chapter is also motivated by

a desire to go beyond the simplistic 'abandon or defend' arguments which some of us, however reluctantly, become ensnared in, whereby the entropic mood of the emboldened sceptic is taken a little too much at face value, and we find ourselves arguing hard in order to stave off theory's death, puffing and panting to resuscitate the dying body, to keep it alive. The irony here being that death, the ineluctable sense of endings, has in a number of different guises been the common denominator in the theoretical work we have sought to champion, to bring to life, over the last twenty years or so. Thus, just as those who oppose theory inadvertently inscribe rather than terminate its time, so those who defend theory necessarily celebrate its death(s). Of course, I am generalising and simplifying the positions that might be taken up around the question of theory's survival – but I do so precisely to demonstrate that, even within the crudest imaginable confrontation, the debate cannot be reduced simply to a matter of out-and-out conflict and opposition. While not wishing to limit the focus of this chapter to the kinds of attitudes and responses that prompted it, what I want to show here is that theory and the commitment (perhaps even resistance) it invites, now and from the outset, cannot therefore merely be a question of living or dying, but always a case of 'living on', surviving 'beyond both living and dying', as Derrida puts it, on the undecidable borderline between the two. I will argue not only that this is (has always been) the place of theory in its interdisciplinarity, but that an understanding of theory's survival along the line(s) charted by Derrida's various discussions of death suggests surviving itself to be the form responsibility takes without measure, without commonplace justification or finally decidable reckoning of the failed and impossible kinds outlined above. To be responsible, contra such positions or approaches, we must understand ourselves as surviving beyond questions of theory's 'life' or 'death' and, through enduring the aporetic nature of such survival, increase the promise and risk of responsibility.

Interdisciplinarity and death

The body without organs is the model of death.

Felix Guattari (with Gilles Deleuze),
'The first positive task of schizoanalysis'[3]

For critical theory and critical theorists, then, death is everywhere. ('Critical theory': itself only ever a so-called thing, something like a phantasm.) The landscape of criticism is thoroughly littered with corpses and ghosts, figures called forth (recalling the motif of resurrection in the midst of a deathly atmosphere) by means of what, by now, might be termed dead metaphors: the last man, the death of the author, the tomb of the intellectual, the end of production and of the social, the culture of death, the end of history and of grand narratives, the university in ruins, the spectres of Marx and even the dying of deconstruction (to name but a few). Even such a list, registering a mortifying compulsion to repeat within its seemingly inexorable forward motion, appears death-driven (the spectral, specular mark of death that engulfs within a reflexive movement both critic and society, the academy and the 'outside world', so that each seem to take on the appearance and attributes of one another in the discourse of these many endings, is an important feature of this). In the names and metonymies of, for example, Hegel, Nietszche, Heidegger, Bataille, Blanchot, Baudrillard, Deleuze, Guattari and Derrida, not to mention the literal as well as the figural deaths of de Man and Foucault, death crosses all frontiers, rearing its head among every relation of nature and culture, the animal and the human, the psyche and the social, the body and the machine, production and consumption, politics and economy, sex and sexuality, past, present and future. In the giddy discourse of 'postmodernism', we might speak of the spiralling velocity of (its) sign value, had we not already shown it to be (and were we not already repeating) an old theme that death is driven to repeat itself everywhere. In fact, in *Specters of Marx*, Derrida remarks somewhat wearily that the eschatological themes of the seemingly countless endings listed above have been around almost as long as anyone can remember, certainly since the 1950s, so that 'the media parade of the current discourse on the end of history and the last man' often takes on the appearance of a repetitive 'tiresome anachronism'.[4] Nevertheless, to dress in modern garb that which is normally recognised as the Freudian story of compulsive repetition, ranged in what Baudrillard calls its 'radical counter-finality' against the disciplined, progressive linearity of the conscious with its limits of reasoned discourse, we might say that, as much as it still lingers, death has become (the figure of the) interdisciplinary.[5] In a way, as Derrida in *Aporias* puts it, 'death does not know any border'.[6] Indeed, to borrow terms from Baudrillard's *Symbolic Exchange and Death*, interdisciplinary work might be viewed as staging the scene of the academic unconscious (itself the unconscious of a modern 'culture of death', perhaps), amounting to the (not classically productive) accumulation of equivalences that cannot be exchanged according to the patrimonial law and utile system of discipline(s) and that, however incalculably, get 'cashed out in the phantasm' – the figure of the unconscious, of general equivalence, that is of death (pp. 146–7).

Just as the so-called postmodern situation is signalled by a plethora of endings, endings limited neither to the limit of the has-been or the to-come, so death from this point of view becomes the haunting figure of the interdisciplinary, the spectre of the neither here nor there, of the *unheimlich*. The veritable life-force that some might see animating the almost viral spread of interdisciplinarity in recent times, unfolding itself as the very sign of a future, has as its uncanny counterpart this always returning spectre of death, this tenaciously ever-present discourse of many endings. However, such a spectre of death cannot be simply opposed and reduced as a mere preoccupation of the present era or moment (a passing whim or a fetish, if you like – although of course such things are never merely of the present moment) or as the very crudest figure of a legacy or inheritance (that is, as something nevertheless recognisably *past* or at least *from* the past: May 1968, for example) since, in Derrida's terms, the spectre not only appears from the first in the form of that which has already come (unworking the reason of a linear temporal scheme) but, in becoming-spectre, always comes *from* the future: 'At bottom, the specter is the future, it is always to come, it presents itself only as that which would come back'.[7] Thus, by way of another equivalence buried deep in the unconsciously compulsive, repetitious pulsions of the interdisciplinary drive – indeed, for thinkers such as Bataille and Baudrillard, the most fundamental equivalence or continuity of life–death – the lively future seemingly promised by the interdisciplinary turn of the last few decades appears inextricably linked with a future bound up with the spectral and the deathly. The spectrality of the interdisciplinary, neither here nor there, dying or bringing death from its first day and at the same time always coming from the future – not least in its promise of surprise – thus turns out to preclude a reckoning of its temporality in the normative terms of a straightforward historical account. In the reading of Derrida that follows, therefore, I suggest but also render finally incalculable, unaccountable, the provenance of interdisciplinarity by locating this in terms of the gift (once more) and death.

Here we might recall some of the arguments made in the previous chapter. As Derrida implies in two essays translated relatively recently, 'The time of the king' and 'The madness of economic reason',[8] it is the discussion of the relationship between gift and exchange found foremost in Mauss's *The Gift* that sparks a vast shift from traditional forms of economism (those predicated on more rudimentary base-superstructure or foreground-background divisions), through anthropology and sociology, structuralism and linguistics, to contemporary cultural study and interdisciplinary work generally in the humanities. Mauss's insistence on the centrality of the concept of the gift, for Derrida, epitomises the pivotal moment at which social thought tries to transcend 'cold economic rationality' by asserting this rationality's 'symbolicity'; thus affording, as Derrida puts it, 'an account of religious, cultural, ideological, discursive, esthetic, literary, poetic phenomena', all organised under the general rubric of the 'economic' (p. 42). Resorting to the gift as a key question within economic thought and reason, then, allows academic discourse to imagine access to the totality of social facts – or, in effect, culture – by rethinking, disposing and deploying the 'economic' within the problem of the gift. As Derrida notes, the gift as formally acknowledged by Mauss's academic study 'gives back, in the place ... of the thing itself, a symbolic equivalent' (pp. 12–13) rendering possible a move from cruder economic determinism and materialism to 'symbolicity' and hence to cultural discourse or a discourse of culture as the regulating site of the modern interdisciplinary humanities and human sciences and the token (paradoxically, in an economy founded through recourse to the gift) of more or less calculated exchanges taking place within them.

If it is the concept of the gift that has allowed the interdisciplinary discourse of culture to come into being, it is important to recognise none the less that the gift is everywhere linked, constellated with death. The gift and death are invariably interwoven motifs in the formations of philosophical and theoretical discourse, meaning and practice that cluster around them. As was noted in Chapter 5, the theme of the sacrificial nature of the gift, described by Mauss in terms of more or less functional collective relations of exchange, reciprocity, obligation, status and deferment within the general economy of archaic societies, returns in the work of Bataille through a shift of emphasis towards a general economy of destructive wastage, of expenditure without reserve, registering absolute loss in excess of the restricted value of any 'return' that individuals or groups might achieve or experience through the potlatch. For Baudrillard, writing in dialogue with Bataille's work to some extent, the productivist, utilitarian tendencies of capitalism have wished exclusion on archaic rituals of loss, sacrifice and the gift, but have nevertheless produced new and unmanageable kinds of surplus and excess, beyond pure use-value or utility, through the spiralling acceleration of sign value within the simulational and semiotic orders developing from the early modern period onwards, causing malfunction as an expression of the system's functions: 'Ours is a society founded on proliferation, on growth which continues even though it cannot be measured against any clear goals ... The upshot is gross systemic congestion and malfunction caused by ... an excess of functional imperatives'.[9] The upshot, in fact, of all these approaches going 'beyond' disciplinary limits – tellingly enough in regard to our discussion of interdisciplinary work itself – is the theme that death inexorably returns within calculative, regulative systems of exchange that cannot ever quite 'cash out' the gift always found to antecede them. Thus, for Baudrillard, the separation and repression of symbolic exchange, the gift and death precipitates a phantasmic return of the excessive and of the other, an other that cannot simply be exorcised through a reasoned exchange or a utilitarian settling of accounts, within political economy. Indeed, just as for Baudrillard in *Symbolic Exchange and Death* 'our entire culture is full of this haunting of the separated double' (p. 142), so we have charted, through a reading of Derrida reading Mauss, the uncanny return of the gift within the reasoned discourse of knowledge and regulated exchange patterns of the academy, the gift being the prime mover of interdisciplinary theory and practice which, by confounding linear and disciplinary schemes, seems death-driven (postmodernism as *post*-modern always comes *from* the future, raising again the figure of the spectre).

In Derrida's even more recent work, *The Gift of Death* for instance, the gift is linked intimately with death in thinking the other, the secret and the question of responsibility. Returning to these themes in an interview conducted to round off the 'Applied Derrida' conference held at the University of Luton in July 1995, Derrida talks of wanting 'to add something, to give something to the other' (here, the explicit context is his philosophical writings 'on Plato, on Kant, on Mallarme and others' that Derrida is often 'reproached for, for not writing anything in my own name'); to countersign 'with my own name' in order to 'be true to the other'.[10] Here the question of responsibility for Derrida is bound up in turn with a reflection on the name 'given' him, and the application of his name in (the name of) deconstruction, not least by young academics who are 'innovative, who are inventing their own way, their own paths' in a 'variety of fields, of topics, of new openings', in effect replaying the interdisciplinary drive under a sign of a 'so-called thing' (deconstruction) that 'started dying from the first day' (pp. 224–5). (In *Aporias*, Derrida speaks of death as a figure 'flashing like a sort of indicator-light (a light at a border) ... between cultures, countries, languages, but also between the areas of knowledge or the disciplines' (pp. 23–4).) It is this application of the name 'Derrida' that formed the theme of the conference itself: 'You can imagine that when one comes to a conference entitled "Applied *You*", you experience the situation in which it is *as if* you were dead' (p. 215) (the very language used here finds Derrida speaking of himself as an other to whom death is applied or *given*). The motifs that consequently recur throughout the interview – itself a closing conversation on the theme of application, in effect on the topic of the opening of borders 'proper' to the (proper) name, the discipline, and so on undertaken through somewhat incalculable patterns of giving and taking – are those of exhaustion, silence (Derrida thanks the conference for tolerating him 'remaining so silent up to now' (p. 213)), the spectral and, finally, 'living on, surviving' (p. 224). (Derrida continues speaking, of course, beyond exhaustion and silence, in an interview where he ponders the fact that he has indeed nevertheless been 'writing a lot' recently! (p. 219).)

Surviving

> Our existence today is marked by a tenebrous sense of survival, living on the borderlines of the 'present'.
>
> Homi K. Bhabha, *The Location of Culture*[11]

What would (what does) it mean – for Derrida, for deconstruction – for theory in its interdisciplinarity to 'live on' among its many endings, to survive the spectre of death, a spectre that seems nevertheless to call it forth, to bring it into being in significant ways? To put the problem in a slightly different form, what could it mean for theory to survive *as* the spectre of death? To live on, *as if* it were dead? There are of course many places we could turn to in Derrida's writing to attempt to formulate some kind of response to such questions. Among his newer work, *Specters of Marx*, by analysing the conjuration of spirit and spectre in Marx, recasts the question of the legacy of Marxism, but also, as Richard Beardsworth has pointed out in *Derrida and the Political*, describes complex processes of the 'spectralisation' of human identity inscribed within an increasingly technicised world, so that here Derrida can be seen as offering 'innovative political reflection' in the face of 'the dynamic of technical processes' that constitute 'political reality today'.[12] Among less recent writing, 'Living on/border lines', by tracing different semantic and syntactic effects in the discussion of what it means to survive, indeed pursuing them to the point of linguistic undecidability and untranslatability, reads 'living on' as from the outset both reprieve and afterlife, triumph *of* life and triumph *over* life, thus recasting death as irreducible supplement so that 'living on goes beyond both living and dying, supplementing each with a sudden surge and a certain reprieve'.[13] Such texts, producing each time different kinds of inflection, offer important insights in terms of both the politics of survival/the survival of politics and living on among the borderlines of meaning, translation, reading, approach, and discipline – the latter raising a whole set of questions that for Derrida are far from simply literary or philosophical ones. These themes will inevitably return in what follows. However, in the context of precisely these sorts of issues, I want in a moment to deploy just a few different examples from Derrida's more recent writing on death, some of it less widely known perhaps than the infamous *Specters of Marx*, to show that, as a problem, 'living on, surviving' in Derrida can be seen to operate on (and indeed expose to questioning) impossibly constituted borders of the very kind that map the place of contemporary theory surviving spectrally in its interdisciplinary formation.

First, however, let us ponder this formation. It may be possible in simple terms to account for interdisciplinary strategies (and counter-strategies) by way of the exchange between the particular and the universal or general, the move from one to the other or the 'to-and-fro' between them. As was noted earlier, interdisciplinary work has often been ventured at locally identified and often unstable frontiers within the field of knowledge, calling for the implementation of plural and heterogeneous forms of theory, methodology and peda-gogy which would have no claim to universal principle or shared value, nor carry any wish to exist as particular expressions of these. All too often, however, a calculable use- and exchange-value has been placed on interdisciplinary difference or 'newness', whereby it becomes recuperable *as* a particular expression of more general formations within the field of knowledge that, not withstanding significant modification and realignment, re-establish transparent norms, spaces of identification and modes of practice with regard to the objects and activity of enquiry. This can be considered somewhat ironic if, as Derrida suggests by way of his reading of Mauss, inter-disciplinarity, in the humanities and human sciences at least, receives its impetus from a gift that can never finally be reckoned up or settled with in relation to the forms and patterns of exchange that it mobilises. Moreover, to return to the question of surviving this seemingly death-driven interdisciplinary work, Derrida's insistence on what he terms the absolute singularity of death renders such an exchange (in the form of an articulation-reconciliation) between the particular and the universal or general finally incalculable. For rather than presenting death simply in terms of the existential struggle of an individuated consciousness *in particular* or as thematic in regard to certain socio-historical or epistemological formations *in general*, Derrida's contemplation of death and survival, as we will see, suspends the relationship between the one and the other and thereby the means of constructing the concept or identity of either. Absolute singularity for Derrida exceeds and unworks the separation of the particular and the universal, and the expression of one in or by means of the other. Yet by scrambling the exchange value of the particular in the universal – thus radically disrupting the normative economy of the institution – Derrida's thought does not simply leave us engulfed by the measureless, specular play of death that subsumes man, intellectuals, authors on the one hand, and history, production, the social on the other. Rather, this 'deprogramming' for Derrida radically opens the question of responsibility in the (deathly) face of the confounded exchange to which absolute singularity subjects the particular and the general and, by extension, the regulation of an interdisciplinary economy of knowledge. To demonstrate this more fully, I want to bring into sharper outline the relevance that Derrida's idea of 'living on', found in his recent work on death, has in relation to this discussion of contemporary academic moves, by contrasting it strategically with Baudrillard's notion of survival within Western modernity found in *Symbolic Exchange and Death*.

This text is interesting and pertinent in the context of Derrida's work on the gift and death to the extent that it explores the relationship between ideas and attitudes concerning mortality and the structure and effects of systems of exchange within various cultural or epistemological formations, in a way which challenges simplistic forms of economic determinism by arguing the primacy of the relation to death in the development of different kinds of exchange patterns. The real reason I have chosen to juxtapose *Symbolic Exchange and Death* with Derrida's work on related issues, however, is that it seems to me to tap into and exemplify longstanding and diverse traditions of intellectual pessimism regarding the increasingly systematised yet ultimately fragmenting political, economic, cultural and semiotic structures and institutions of modern mass society. This pessimism permeates the culture and civilisation tradition that we associate with Arnold and Leavis, establishes the

tone of much European modernism, and solidifies in the more sys-
tematic theoretical work of key figures of the Frankfurt School. It is
recorded in the impact of critics like Richard Hoggart upon the
formation of cultural studies and, despite the resistance offered by
more optimistic, celebratory approaches to popular culture in recent
times, returns today in the endless debates over postmodernism.
In *Symbolic Exchange and Death* this pessimistic tendency is
captured in Baudrillard's image of the restricted and deadening
forms of survival that constitute 'life' within the political economy
of late capitalism. For Derrida, in contrast, 'living on' exposes the
systemic formations of modernity, not least within the field of
knowledge, to their own limits and limitations. Thus 'living on'
exists not merely as an expression of the system's functions but also
constitutes a form of deconstruction. This offers, if not simply an
alternative, a different sort of approach and enablement than is
found in the pessimistic thinking which – as in Baudrillard's text –
often attends images of twentieth-century life as a form of survival.

Derrida's idea of 'living on' is therefore dissimilar in important
ways to the kind of survival which for Baudrillard results from the
exclusion within political economy of the incessant play of symbolic
exchange with death found in archaic societies. In *Symbolic
Exchange and Death*, survival is imagined as a fundamentally alienated kind of '*residual* life' lived in finite, linear time as a sort of calculated accumulation of surplus-value paid for by 'the ever-present
phantasm of death'. Baudrillard writes: 'In survival, death is
repressed; life itself, in accordance with that well known ebbing
away, would be nothing more than a survival determined by death'
(pp. 127–33). In the context of an encounter with Heidegger in *The
Gift of Death*, Derrida speaks of the irreducible singularity of death
in a way that begins to problematise Baudrillard's image of survival.
Here, Derrida asserts the absolute singularity of death according to
formulations which raise and, indeed, bewilder the question of
exchange that is central to Baudrillard's classification of different
cultural and historical relationships to death: 'Because I cannot take
death away from the other who can no more take it from me in
return, it remains for everyone to take his own death *upon himself*';
'no one can die in my place or in the place of the other'.[14] However
grounded in the language or presence of the 'I' such formulations

might seem, they do not simply evoke the particularity of the individual expressed as synecdoche or sovereign example in relation to the (fictional) generality of, for instance, Western democratic law. This expressive relationship in fact provides the model for the dichotomous articulation of an alienated/autonomous 'individual fatality' which, in survival of the kind presented by Baudrillard, 'weighs down on life' excluded from universal symbolic exchange (p. 132). In *The Gift of Death*, however, 'living on' in the face of the absolute singularity of death occurs in a way that both dispels an expressive relation to a general other and effectively surpasses any calculated economic exchange of time as a surplus-value extracted from death. Thus, Derrida insists, 'I can die for the other in a situation where my death gives him a little longer to live' but 'I cannot die in her place, I cannot give my life in exchange for her death' (p. 43). Here, the separation of the particular ('my death') from the general (the death of the other, to the extent of all other deaths) – a separation in which Baudrillard locates the repression of symbolic exchange and, consequently, workaday survival – is entirely unworked due to the *impossibility* of an exchange (articulation-reconciliation) between the two. In Derrida's ensuing discussion concerning the 'sacrifice' of Isaac, one that pays close attention to Kierkegaard's *Fear and Trembling*, the singularity of the event, beyond ethics, duty or reason, brings about the impossibility of this exchange in the form of the aporia of responsibility and not simply to the effect of responsibility's absence which, as we will see, Baudrillard associates with the modern, rational system which one only mundanely survives. For Derrida, the demand such as that placed upon Abraham to answer or account for oneself in particular before the (fictional) community or the general, to translate the event into reasoned language through a commonly measured exchange 'one-for-the-other', introduces 'the idea of substitution' which dilutes the 'uniqueness' and 'absolute singularity' both of the 'sacrifice' demanded by God and the unmitigated responsibility it places on Abraham's shoulders (p. 61). As Kierkegaard puts it, 'Abraham *cannot* speak, because he cannot say that which would explain everything'.[15] Thus, through respect for 'nonsubstitution, nonrepetition', responsibility in its absolute form is bound to 'silence and secrecy', so that a *concept* of responsibility cannot be presented or its application measured (in a transaction between the particular and universal) according to law, ethics, reason or duty (pp. 60–3). From this point of view, far from evoking a sort of individual fatality survived only by extracting the surplus-value of finite time from a death 'outside' symbolic exchange and thus separated from life, the singularity of death in Derrida's discussion places its survivor(s) at the limits of calculated exchange, contract or reasoned discourse. Here, the polarising and reabsorbative moves of political economy (of a kind with the regulated formation of interdisciplinary knowledge) break down. Yet at the same time such limits create a space for the question of responsibility to arise once more, for Derrida absolutely in the form of the 'impossible'.

Elsewhere in his writing, the aporias Derrida discovers in the Heideggerian philosophical discourse of existence (*Dasein*) finding itself in the possibility of an impossibility (death *as such*) show that his contemplation of death does not return us intact to 'the dialectic of a conscious subject' or a disciplined exchange between the individual/particular and the general that Baudrillard associates with the 'Enlightenment thinkers', with both scientific rationalism and existential despair, and by extension with the anguished yet profoundly mundane survival of modernity (p. 190). Rather, for Derrida, the undecidability of the point of departure from which an existential analysis of death might be embarked upon precludes the normative coherence and rational unity of an ego, person, subject, or indeed discipline. Instead, this undecidability figures being-toward-death in terms akin to the non-self-identical structure of the *unheimlich* and presents survival itself (and *not* that which it excludes) in the indeterminate form of the phantasm. Derrida's essay 'Awaiting (at) the arrival' explores the issue of whether the 'proper' contemplation of death begins from here, 'on this side', or there, on the 'other side', of the limit or border of death. For Derrida, 'this side' is implicitly taken as the point of departure in Heidegger's *Being and Time* for existential analysis to distinguish an opposition between the other side (that which pertains to theology or a metaphysics of 'immortality, the beyond') and this side (the side primarily of psychological and anthropological investigations and of ethical, juridicial and political norms regulating the question of 'what one should do or think *down here* before death'). Paradoxically enough, however, 'this side' is also chosen by Heidegger as a position from which to subsume and transcend the opposition, to situate existential analysis as 'anterior, neutral and independent' in relation to the presupposed concept(s) of death constituting 'problematic closure' on both sides (pp. 44–53). In contrast, Derrida shows how Levinas thinks the question of death from the other side or, at least, from the side of the other: the impossibility *as such* of death as the absolute law of the 'there' means that *Dasein*'s possibility, found in its relation to death, must always be mediated by the other. For Levinas, as Derrida puts it, 'the death of the other is the first death' (p. 39), a death which the mortal must face with responsibility insofar as he is mortal, recalling the problem of respect for the other as nevertheless a kind of alter ego (one's other self) found in Derrida's essay on Levinas's thought, 'Violence and metaphysics'.[16]

However, for Derrida, Levinas and Heidegger cannot simply be opposed, this side against that. Rather, by reading Heidegger somewhat against himself, Derrida finds a certain undecidedness concerning the 'here' as a point of departure. The Heideggerian affinity with 'this side', rendered at the same time necessary and untenable by the impossibility of recognising, delimiting, affirming the other side *as such*, is further unsettled since existential analysis in any case locates itself in an 'anterior, neutral, and independent' place that supposedly pre-exists a decision between one side and the other. This undecidedness allows a position to be worked from which Derrida can say, 'Death, the most proper possibility of *Dasein*, is the possibility of a being-able-no-longer-to-be-there or of a no-longer-being-able-to-be-there as *Dasein*' (p. 68). Here, the approach of existential analysis is located only with some anxiety in the place of the 'here' (this side) since the proper possibility of *Dasein* as the possibility of an impossibility (existence affirming itself in death *as such*) is removed to 'there', the other side. This move nevertheless remains unachievable *as such*, Derrida tells us, since the possibility of *Dasein* is inextricably linked to the inability of itself to *be* 'there': 'there' being death. As 'here' here impossibly becomes 'there', in a move that recalls the uncanny, the spectre and (its) disjointed time explored in *Specters of Marx*, being-toward-death is thought without recourse to the reasoned, decisive borderlines of 'an ego or egological sameness' (p. 39) or disciplined subject that projects and excludes all that ostensibly falls 'outside' itself. Instead, for Derrida, the existential analysis of death inevitably gives rise to the consideration of 'mourning and ghosting [*revenance*], spectrality or living on, surviving, as non-derivable categories or as non-reducible derivations' (p. 61). These categories or derivations are, according to Derrida, ineliminable in the aporetic nature of the Heideggerian philosophy of *Dasein*. In a certain way, that is, they survive it. But they do so in a form which resolutely is not assimilable to the work of a conscious project, a calculated exchange, a discipline or, one might say, a final decision.

This spectral image of 'living on' as the figure (indeed as the consequence) of an irreducible aporia, then, has quite different implications from Baudrillard's idea of survival as the disciplined, calculated extraction of surplus-value, in the form of finite time, from death. Yet it also differs significantly from Baudrillard's presentation of death (*not* survival) returning as the repressed figure of the exclusions and separations brought about by political economy, scientific rationalism and (post-)Enlightenment discipline. As we have seen, the spectrality of 'living on, surviving' arises in *Aporias* not from an historically categorised model of repression and return but through the extreme undecidability of the 'here' and the 'there'. This radically disrupts the somewhat normative temporal scheme found in Baudrillard's analysis of the rise of modernity, given by way of historical/conceptual classifications of, for example, the primitive order and political economy, which if not hermetically bounded are none the less effectively ordered and juxtaposed as distinctive, consecutive formations.[17] The effect of thinking the question of death/survival in terms of the extreme undecidability of 'here' and 'there', as Derrida does, rather than by way of a *temporally determined logic* of repression and return (amounting in effect to a history at the ends of history) is not to advance, outside of time and in neglect of the complex temporalisations of Heideggerian thought,[18] an ahistoricist philosophy of heroic struggle with death as, for example, the apogee of a general human condition. Again, this would depend on the decisive division and expression of particular and universal whereas, as Beardsworth puts it, deconstruction deconstructs 'the empirico-transcendental difference' and thereby 'releases time and singularity from logical determination'.[19] Rather, by putting the question of being-toward-death (and of survival) in terms of the aporia or impossibility of absolute decisiveness in regard to singularity and time, Derrida crucially (re)opens the issue of responsibility which he argues can only arise in the face of the undecided, itself linked to a less conceptually determined sense of the temporal. This temporality is presented by Derrida, in *Specters of Marx* for instance, in terms of a disjointed 'now' suffused with the *differance* of time. From a deconstructive viewpoint, this would be the aspect of time that gets lost in Baudrillard's – however perverse and perversely Freudian – categorised history in *Symbolic Exchange and Death*. Thus, no doubt unsurprisingly for Derrida, the possibility of being responsible is – in an instance of deciding between, opposing, expressing the relation of 'here' and 'there', 'now' and 'then', the particular (individualistic survival within political economy) and the universal (symbolic exchange in the primitive order) – utterly discounted by Baudrillard as an 'illogical' historical anachronism. Baudrillard writes, 'responsibility has been dead a long time. As a vestigial individual trait from the Enlightenment, it has been eliminated by the system itself as the latter becomes more *rational*' (p. 170). Ironically, then, a decisive separation and exclusion of death, in the form of long-dead responsibility, is performed here by Baudrillard himself. In contrast, since Derrida's discussion locates (survives) the aporia of death in the undecidability of 'here' and 'there', of 'this side' and the other, it remains irreducible to any conceptualised or historicised (logical) separation of the rational and irrational – not least within the effectively normalising temporal scheme that, as in the quote from Baudrillard above, finds itself able to identify and delimit anachronisms as exceptions to an otherwise compelling historical rule. Indeed, we might wonder how an anachronism, which exists in relation to the borders of time as profoundly and tenaciously a figure of trangressive possibility, can simply be located and fixed in terms of the historical limits of an era or epoch. Does not its very 'illogicality' shatter the epochal determination of the 'rational' as an historical 'system' that Baudrillard is bound to uphold in order to deride and invert it? (A much more far-reaching sense of anachrony as the condition of thoroughly disjointed time arises in Derrida's contemplation of the figure of the spectre in *Specters of Marx*.) From a Derridean point of view, then, the question of responsibility – located in the aporia or undecidability of death's 'here-or-there-ness' – survives the kind of separations, exclusions and divisions central to Baudrillard's thinking of the problem of death, so that it is neither, on the one hand, simply outmoded in view of an evermore rational system nor, on the other, simply anomalous in relation to anti-rationalism (for example, in regard to the deradicalised nihilism sometimes found in Baudrillard[20]).

Here, then, (and this is the point of my sustaining a focus on those parts of Derrida's work on Heidegger that are in tension with Baudrillard) the responsibility that arises from Derrida's thinking on the problem of death locates itself neither inside nor outside, neither here nor there, but on the fraying borders of the systemic, the rational, the discipline(d): the very place where theory survives its interdisciplinary formation. And in fact this borderline or limit remains perpetually unsettled, undecided, as the very condition of what Derrida might term theory's promise, its future in the form of an always impossible possibility: just as responsibility (rather than the deradicalised nihilism of Baudrillard) is, for Derrida, called forth by a death it can never fully comprehend, delimit, answer for or finish with, so interdisciplinary theory receives its charge from a gift it can never finally reckon or settle with in regard to the patterns of exchange that this sets in motion. Indeed, to reorder this Derridean formulation: the interdisciplinary turn brought about by incalculable recourse to the gift drives theory towards a death from which it nevertheless receives measureless responsibility. This, I believe, is at least one way of reading Derrida on survival and the responsibility of survival.

As such/as if

I would like to see what it looks like *as if* I were dead.

Jacques Derrida, '*As if* I were dead'[21]

If Baudrillard insists upon the inevitable return of the gift and death as that which cannot ever be entirely 'cashed out' by rational, disciplined, systemic exchanges of the kind we might locate in the political economy of a regulated interdisciplinarity, by nevertheless renouncing the possibility of responsibility before, outside of – but also after, within – this return, he effectively depoliticises survival on the 'borderlines of the "present"'. By suggesting that the question of responsibility is irrelevant both in relation to the present system and a future 'beyond' it, Baudrillard risks re-inscribing the political and ideological constraints surrounding the inert forms of survival he wishes to expose and critique. On the other hand, by offering a way to situate the impetus and development of interdisciplinary theory in terms of the themes and problems of the gift and death, deconstruction opens on to a survival 'beyond' logical determination. For Derrida, this would take shape not on the other side of the rational (the irrational or anti-rational) but on the impossibly constituted borders of the disciplinary and systemic. Thus, in Derridean terms, the inconceivable chance of absolute responsibility would be released where theory most sustains its interdisciplinarity, fulfilling itself by never fulfilling itself, never finishing itself, 'living on ... beyond both living and dying ... a sudden surge and a certain reprieve'. (This unfinishedness at the limits of logical determination or orientation would of course produce very different effects than those we identified with the closely regulated mobile horizon – the very paradigm – of enlightenment/censorship in Chapter 4.) It is in the release from logical determination of time and singularity (this 'from' carries a multiple syntactical charge) that Richard Beardsworth locates the possibilities of both a deconstruction of politics and the 'political' thrust of deconstruction. Through its aporetic 'relation' to the irresolvable problems of the gift and death, releasing singularity and time from logical determinants, I would argue that theory in its interdisciplinarity is capable of and well equipped for just such a 'political' move.

The merits of such a claim could only be established, however, through a sustained engagement with Beardsworth's argument concerning the deconstruction of normative political reality brought about by way of a powerfully charged rethinking of its models of time and place. While there is not the space to attempt that here, I want to contribute in a small way to Beardsworth's insights by concluding with a few remarks on the syntactical weight of *as if* in the linguistic construction by which Derrida contemplates the relationship to death. Clearly this is not posited as simply an alternative to, an exit from, the impossible possibility of death *as such* found in Heidegger's *Being and Time*. Instead, *as if* suspends itself in the aporetic space, as it were, of the existential analysis of death. Derrida argues that to 'relate to an object *as such* means to relate to it as if you were dead'; that is, to suppose the object as it is 'when you are not there'.[22] The upshot of this fantasy of grasping the objectivity or truth of an object or, indeed, an other is the experience of being 'quasi-dead' (recalling the Levinasian theme that the relation to death, however unachievable, is received from the other.) The very condition, then, of the impossible possibility of *as such* is *as if*. Put in Derridean language, *as if* is the supplement, the inexhaustible and incalculable remainder that can neither be left out nor 'cashed out', of the *as such*. In the form of *as if*, an aporia of articulation returns, suspended, from the impossible possibility of *as such*. Beardsworth associates the term 'aporia' (in its Derridean usage, at least) with an idea of the impassable. Similarly, through its *play* with the literal, the analogical does not function in a straightforward way to illuminate that which exists outside itself, as an instance or example of an object or entity or an exploration or *application* of a first principle. Rather, the analogue offers an intralinguistic deixis, an indication which, as Giorgio Agamben has put it, 'does not simply demonstrate an unnamed object, but above all the very instance of discourse, its taking place'.[23] Simplistically, analogies might therefore be thought to be different from 'conventional' language, that is in its representational normativity. Yet, as Derrida shows, they remain everywhere embedded in it as a necessary condition of language itself: the *as if* is always the upshot of the *as such*. As if in its non-self-identicality, its *unheimlich* 'neither-here-nor-thereness', thus survives as the irreducible supplement of language – that is, in an originary 'relation' to it. *As if* always begins by coming back, is always spectral. *As if* is always in some sense the *as if* of a death that takes us beyond living or dying.

For Derrida, for deconstruction, for criticism in its interdisciplinarity 'living on' impossibly constituted borders 'beyond' logical determination, *as if* – neither simply this nor that, living nor dead, authentic nor simulated – is irreducibly to be endured (though, of course, never *as such*) in the many 'deaths' of theory. Yet in enduring it, *as if* offers the chance to redeem language from representational deadness, to release politics from the logically determined calculation and reduction of differences, to deconstruct the identities of time and place that constitute the construction of predominant forms of political reality. In this way (as Derrida would perhaps put it) interdisciplinary theory, surviving *as if* it were dead, might take responsibly the gift of itself beyond reckoning.

Notes

1 Jacques Derrida, '*As if* I were dead: an interview with Jacques Derrida', in *Applying: To Derrida*, ed. John Brannigan, Ruth Robbins and Julian Wolfreys (London: Macmillan, 1996), pp. 224–5.

2 See Nicholas Royle, *After Derrida* (Manchester: Manchester University Press, 1995), p. 1.

3 Felix Guattari (with Gilles Deleuze), 'The first positive task of schizoanalysis', in *The Guattari Reader*, ed. Gary Genosko (Oxford: Basil Blackwell, 1996).

4 Jacques Derrida, *Specters of Marx: The State of the Debt, the Work of Mourning, and the New International*, trans. Peggy Kamuf (London: Routledge,1994), p. 15.

5 Jean Baudrillard, *Symbolic Exchange and Death*, trans. Iain Hamilton Grant (London: Sage, 1993), p. 149. All further references will be given in the main body of the text.

6 Jacques Derrida, *Aporias: Dying – Awaiting (One Another At) the 'Limits of Truth'*, trans. Thomas Dutoit (California: Stanford University Press, 1993), p. 57. All further references will be given in the main body of the text.

7 Jacques Derrida, *Specters of Marx*, p. 39.

8 Jacques Derrida, *Given Time: 1. Counterfeit Money*, trans. Peggy Kamuf (Chicago, IL and London: University of Chicago Press, 1992), pp. 1–33; pp. 34–70. All further references will be given in the main body of the text.

9 Jean Baudrillard, *The Transparency of Evil: Essays on Extreme Phenomena* (London: Routledge, 1993), p. 31.

10 Derrida, '*As if* I were dead', p. 220. All further references in this section of the chapter will be given in the main body of the text.

11 Homi K. Bhabha, *The Location of Culture* (London and New York: Routledge, 1994), p. 1.

12 Richard Beardsworth, *Derrida and the Political* (London: Routledge, 1996), pp. 146–8. It might be possible to relate this aspect of *Specters of Marx* to Derrida's reflections on death and the machine in his earlier essay 'Freud and the scene of writing', in *Writing and Difference*, trans. Alan Bass (London: Routledge, 1995), pp. 196–231: 'The machine is dead. It is death.

Not because we risk death in playing with machines, but because the origin of machines is the relation to death' (p. 227). In this connection see also Geoffrey Bennington, 'Aberrations: de Man (and) the machine', in *Reading de Man Reading*, ed. Lindsay Waters and Wlad Godzich (Minneapolis, MN: University of Minnesota Press, 1989).

13 Jacques Derrida, 'Living on/border lines', in *Deconstruction and Criticism*, ed. Geoffrey Hartman (London and Henley: Routledge and Kegan Paul, 1979), see p. 108.

14 Jacques Derrida, *The Gift of Death*, trans. David Wills (Chicago, IL and London: University of Chicago Press, 1995) p. 44. All further references will be given in the main body of the text. See also *Aporias*, p. 22.

15 Cited in Jacques Derrida, *The Gift of Death*, p. 61. Derrida quotes from Søren Kierkegaard, *Fear and Trembling, and Repetition, Volume 6, Kierkegaard's Writings* (Princeton, NJ: Princeton University Press, 1983), p. 115.

16 Jacques Derrida, 'Violence and metaphysics: an essay on the thought of Emmanuel Levinas', in *Writing and Difference*, pp. 79–153.

17 It might be objected that Baudrillard's thought presents history, at the 'end of history' in the late twentieth century, as pure simulacra, thus identifying the historical with the endless proliferation of simulation to the extent of the disappearance of any kind of normative temporality or linear or teleological scheme. See for example Richard Bogard, 'Baudrillard, time, and the end', in *Baudrillard: A Critical Reader*, ed. Douglas Kellner (Oxford: Basil Blackwell, 1995) pp. 313–33. Such detachment from historical finitude or finality within the orders of hyperreality, simulation and precession (which Bogard associates with 'repetition in advance') seems utterly to disconcert the paradigms of traditional history. However, as Bogard himself suggests, 'the disappearance of historical time' appears 'endlessly bound up with the idea of history and sequential time'. Simulation and hyperreality as void of history (except, of course, as simulation and hyperreality) are therefore nevertheless always of 'the modern age'. On the one hand, the historical past is entirely simulated within the modern order of things; on the other, Baudrillard often (as in *Symbolic Exchange and Death*) tends to accord the past – even a mythic, fictionalised past – a different kind of agency by using it to explain or at least attend to the emergence and formation of the reflexivity of the modern. Hence, Bogard concedes that it has been 'difficult' for Baudrillard to 'break with the sense of historical anticipation and determination' accompanying 'the question of ends' that pervades his work (p. 328).

18 See Richard Beardsworth, *Derrida and the Political*, pp. 104–14.

19 *Ibid.*, p. 146.

20 The term 'deradicalised nihilism' is based on (and deliberately skews) claims found in Bogard's essay. Here he argues that, for Baudrillard, the system

cannot fundamentally be challenged by a 'radical indifference to meaning or value' – that is, a conventional form of nihilism – since it itself steals a march on the nihilistic enterprise by functioning as an order that in fact 'radicalises nihilism to the point of its own reversion, its own de-radicalisation' (p. 316). While Bogard argues that Baudrillard attempts to explore different modes of thought going beyond now deradicalised 'conventional' nihilism, I would argue that Baudrillard's 'nihilism' itself becomes deradicalised at the moment the system is seen as exhaustive, albeit implosive; and destined, albeit open to Baudrillardian speculation or 'betting'.

21 Jacques Derrida, '*As if* I were dead', p. 215.
22 *Ibid.*, p. 216.
23 Georgio Agamben, *Language and Death: The Place of Negativity*, trans. Karen E. Pinkus and Michael Hardt (Minneapolis, MN: University of Minnesota Press, 1991) quoted in Ronald Schleifer, 'Afterword: Walter Benjamin and the crisis of representation: multiplicity, meaning, and athematic death', in *Death and Representation*, ed. Sarah Webster Goodwin and Elisabeth Bronfen (Baltimore and London: The Johns Hopkins University Press, 1993), p. 321.

The art of memory

So far, so near an apparent end, things may still seem a little inconclusive. Where were we? (At one and the same time, in a disorienting way, this means: where are we now? but also: where have we been?) Let's try to remember.

In the vicinity of a number of different issues and contexts ranging across the past, present and future of the modern academic institution, I have suggested an intractable problem of disorientation in the university that nevertheless provides the conditions for certain kinds of leverage to occur. At times such leverage produces rather disasterously confused effects confounding the intention with which it was undertaken. Not least, the taking up of a supposed position of opposition in relation to the 'object' that one wishes to lever against frequently entails a sort of repudiation or disavowal of the very conditions under which leverage can occur. The lever is used to exert force against the body which resists it, but nevertheless operates only by means of that 'other' body's own pressure. As the university walks on two feet (two feet which may not amount to a pair, but a monstrously non-self-identical double) the momentum that impels one 'side' or 'foot' relies wholly on the leverage received from the other. Yet the disorientation that is frequently compounded in the exercise of institutional leverage does not altogether rule out or exclude a somewhat more affirmative response to the unstable, even impossible, conditions in which the university can be found(ed). In the blinking of an eye; thinking 'without identity' amid the university's deconstructible walls and the uneven rhythms of (disciplinary) attachment and detachment; in a situation of dis-re-pair in which the institution finds, founds, foots itself – survival tactics present themselves. Survival itself happens inconclusively, beyond logical determination, neither simply useful nor useless, here nor there, alive nor dead. Systematically incapable of closure, this survival – rather like a gift to today's interdisciplinarian academics – survives the measure of excellence. All this means, however, that survival cannot be conclusively marked as either negative or positive. Instead survival, like the surplus-mark of an instituted division, belongs to neither side of the division that it endures.

I am gathering together in the properly (improper) monstrous motif of survival, then, a diverse and disparate array of bits from deconstruction's body of texts. Survival springs up in the vicinity of the institution's limits and divisions (rather like literature or deconstruction, perhaps): stitched together at these very limits, it ultimately belongs – however improperly, as a figure of dis-re-pair – to the interlacing of *differance* rather than the logic of a cut. The survival tactics of this book have something to do with the way in which, instead of presenting a sturdy and comprehensive account of the university's historical genealogy, its intellectual history and 'actual' formation within and across a series of different models, it is sown together out of bits and pieces found at the apparent edges of the institution: Van Gogh's shoes, the 'glasse' of Renaissance kingship, the *New Atlantis*, the multiple submissions debate, the uncanny return of the gift amid the calculated exchanges of a generalised interdisciplinarity, survival itself. Rather than simply denying or seeking to overcome disorienting effects, my project is therefore to attempt to practice a sort of disorientation in the form of disorienting somewhat the question of the university itself: specifically the question of what is central and what is peripheral to this question, what lies inside or outside it, what is merely a circuitous delay, an unfocused meander, and what is a direct route to the problem of the university institution. Amid this kind of disorientation, it will never do simply to engage the somewhat formal procedures of inversion or reversal with regard to the conceptual distinctions and oppositions that would seem to define the characteristic features of the university institution after Enlightenment. The disorientation discovered and practised in this book demands, more profoundly, a responsibility and responsiveness at the very limits of the university's possibility, giving rise to new sorts of orientation somewhat along the lines of Heidegger's insistence on taking a step within the circle. Perhaps one way of imagining this 'new', disorienting kind of orientation would be to take a detour once again through the question of history and of memory insofar as it relates to the institution of the institution.

In 'The art of *memoires*', the second in a series of three lectures given in memory of Paul de Man, Derrida draws attention to de Man's strong reading of Hegel's *Aesthetics*. Here are found difficult and discontinuous elements that, as de Man puts it, 'cannot be resolved by the canonical system explicitly established by Hegel himself, namely the dialectic'.[1] Allegory features strongly as a difficult problem to dismiss within the dialectical system. In the very terms of the dialectic itself, 'what appears to be inferior and enslaved … may well turn out to be master … just as … neglected corners in the Hegelian canon are perhaps masterful articulations'.[2] In Derrida's eyes, what is happening here is that:

> Paul de Man *appears to be playing* a supplement of dialectic against the untrue dialectic; he seems to play at reminding us what *must be remembered*, must be recalled to vigilance, called to life, recalled to good memory against bad dozing memory, against the dogmatic slumbers of a tradition … [but] what he ultimately wants us to recall is not the good-living-memory but on the contrary the essential mutual implication of thought and of what the tradition defines as 'bad' memory.[3]

What must be remembered, what must survive, is not simply 'good-living-memory' over and against, unbound by, freed from, the 'dogmatic slumbers of a tradition'. Instead, thought happens precisely at the point where recollection can be portrayed by a 'tradition' as '"bad" memory'. Not quite excluded and not quite included, '"bad" memory' encapsulates, according to Derrida's reading of de Man, 'the art of memory', which is to think 'at the boundaries', indeed to think the boundary, 'the limit of interiority' (p. 71). Thus I have shyed away from any attempt to recollect a better memory of the university, one that is more broad and capacious, more smoothly coherent, less prone to factual error than previous memories have been. Instead I have stitched together the pieces of this book (in the way that Frankenstein's creature was made) as a kind of persistent bad memory. I suppose for some who might find it excessively difficult, seemingly discontinuous, totally unfounded, it is a sort of nightmare. In the blink of an eye, neither simply hard eyed and vigilant nor blindly asleep, this vision of the university is interimplicated with whatever 'tradition' might identify it as 'bad': that is to say, it crops up in the vicinity of debates, histories and mission statements concerning the university such that any question put to this '"bad" memory' is also necessarily a question for the 'tradition' itself. I would hope therefore that the vision of the university glimpsed in this book encourages not just approval or agreement but dissensual thought, that it spurs not just a better recollection but the art of memory.

Returning to Derrida's reading of de Man's reading of Hegel's *Aesthetics*, we find that allegory narrates, in Hegel's terms, 'the separation of subject and predicate'.[4] 'For discourse to be meaningful, this separation has to take place,' writes de Man. Yet the very same separation is 'incompatible with the necessary generality of meaning' in the Hegelian dialectical system. Thus allegory 'functions, categorically and logically, like the defective cornerstone of the entire system'. Derrida pauses at this point in de Man's text to note that here, in this 'architectural rhetoric', we find 'a figure of what some might be tempted to see as the dominant metaphorical register' of deconstruction (p. 72). According to the standard view usually afforded by this architectural imagery, deconstruction sets out to locate in the system that it analyses the 'defective cornerstone', the frequently hidden yet structurally indispensable support for the generality of the system, its entire architectonics, that nevertheless 'threatens the coherence and the internal order of the construction'. Here, at the often unseen, self-deconstructing limits of the grand edifice, would seem to be 'the best spot for efficiently inserting the deconstructive lever,' notes Derrida. This kind of levering against the cornerstone is something that seems to be underway in my own 'bad memory' of the university edifice, in that the lever in my various analyses is inserted near the cornerstone, at the barely visible edges of the institution's framework, rather than in the proximity of any keystone. The latter, Derrida tells us, would be 'a central, commanding point' (p. 74): for example, along with Bill Readings, we might identify reason or culture as keystones of the academic institution after Enlightenment. But, on Readings' account, in the dereferentialised university of excellence, devoid of a content or a centre, there can be no keystone to lever against. We are left only with the (defective) cornerstone, the decentred support, a little out of the way, perhaps even a little separate or detached (rather like an allegory), that none the less simultaneously upholds and threatens the generality of meaning of the system.

However, suddenly and surprisingly, Derrida exclaims that 'Paul de Man's "deconstructive" moves do not at all obey this logic or this "architectural" rhetoric' (p. 73). This is in no small part due to the fact that deconstruction, far from being tied to the architectural figure that seems to occupy its very name, actually disputes 'the constructionist account' of itself. To put it in de Manian terms, the archictectural rhetoric so frequently used to build a framework within which to comprehend deconstruction is itself allegorical. The entire rhetorical ensemble of the edifice, the framework, the structure, the keystone, the cornerstone and even the lever turn out to be part of a (necessarily defective) allegorical system which, if it is allegorical, cannot be thought of constructionistically, as it were. Perhaps this is why, in the Genet column of *Glas*, Derrida discovers what he terms 'the good metaphor' for describing his (in Simon Critchley's phrase) 'interpretative practice'[5] – that of the dredging machine:

> I am seeking the good movement. Have I constructed something like the matrix ...? No, I see rather (but it may still be a matrix or a grammar) a sort of dredging machine. From the dissimulated, small, closed, glassed-in cabin of a crane, I manipulate some levers and ... I plunge a mouth of steel in the water. And I scrape the bottom, hook onto stones and algae there that I lift up in order to set them down on the ground while the water quickly falls back from the mouth.[6]

Penned into the dredging machine, still possibly 'a matrix or a grammar', a constructionist system or an architectural-technological structure, Derrida manipulates some levers which, far from bringing up the entire basis or fabric of the sea, allow a watery silt to, as Critchley puts it, 'slip through the teeth of the reading machine and *remain*'. Even if, at times, deconstruction cannot help operating within a constructionist model of itself, Derrida in *Glas* recognises that the deconstructive levers pulled within any such machine-like model or framework leave aside a remains (just as allegory as a difficult problem or discontinuous element cannot easily be resolved within Hegel's dialectical system, and just as the instituted divisions of the university leave always a surplus-mark). The 'good metaphor' of the dredging machine and of the lever therefore consists in letting the remains remain, letting them survive as remains. To this extent, in fact, the 'good metaphor' militates against a complacently constructionist account or practice of deconstruction which is itself always strongly allegorical or figural. In these terms, paradoxically, the 'good metaphor' of the lever is good precisely to the extent that, while it allows the remains (for example, of allegory) to remain, it becomes, as it were, less metaphorical. It becomes itself the remains, the surplus-mark that exceeds and survives any distinction between the so-called figural and the so-called structural.

For de Man allegory remains, both 'before and after Hegel', in a way that makes possible the concept and the construction of history. Thus, Derrida tells us, one cannot simply 'rely on something like history', the concept of which is in fact an effect of the allegorical, 'to account for this "allegoricity"' (p. 74). According to the line of thought we are following here, allegory would be the remains of history on which, nevertheless, history is founded. A conventional, more or less empirical historical account – of the university institution for instance – would always, despite itself, be founded on these remains although it could never hope to master, resolve, supersede or expel them. Yet any 'interpretative practice' that let these remains remain, thereby hastening the reversal or inversion of the master-slave relations of the dialectic and the allegorical, would not simply abadon itself to the figural. As I noted in my introduction, the apparent lack of literalism, empiricism or historical reference that would characterise at least parts of this book does not mean that the title should be qualified by a term such as 'figuratively speaking'. If it is the conventional concept and construction of history that depends most heavily on the very allegoricity it seeks to denounce, repel or deny, then rather like the 'good metaphor' of the lever in *Glas*, a study of the university which allowed the remains to remain would in fact be less metaphorical than the most literal, referential account ever written. To this extent, it might even be more historical than the most conventionally historical narrative one could imagine. As a kind of '"bad" memory', it would revive the art of memory forgotten by history itself.

Notes

1 Paul de Man, 'Reply to Raymond Geuss', *Critical Inquiry* (December 1983) 389–90, quoted in Jacques Derrida, 'The art of *memoires*', in his *Memoires for Paul de Man*, revised edition (New York: Columbia University Press, 1989), p. 68.

2 Paul de Man, 'Sign and symbol in Hegel's *Aesthetics*', *Critical Inquiry* (Summer 1982) 774–5, quoted in 'The art of *memoires*', p. 70.

3 Jacques Derrida, 'The art of *memoires*', pp. 45–88, see pp. 70–1. All further references will be given in the main body of the text.

4 Paul de Man, 'Sign and symbol in Hegel's *Aesthetics*', quoted in 'The art of *memoires*', p. 72.

5 Simon Critchley, *Very Little ... Almost Nothing: Death, Philosophy, Literature* (London and New York: Routledge, 1997), p. 146.

6 Jacques Derrida, *Glas* (Lincoln, NB and London: University of Nebraska Press, 1990), p. 204.

Index of names

Note: 'n.' after a page number refers to a note on that page.